JACQUELI...

FOREWORD BY BISHOP EDDIE L. LONG

I Wasn't Born This Way

A TESTIMONY OF
SPIRITUAL RENEWAL
AND WHOLENESS

Published by Solex Publishing, a division of Solex Enterprises LLC
Fayetteville, GA 30214

Unless otherwise indicated, all Scripture quotations in this book are from the King James Versions®

Designed by Solex Enterprises
soloed@mindspring.com

"I WASN'T BORN THIS WAY!"

A Testimony of Spiritual Renewal
From
Brokeness to Wholeness

By
Jacqueline R. Lamar

Genesis 1:27 - "So God created man in his own image, in the image of God created he him: male and female created he them".

Foreword by
Bishop Eddie L. Long

"And they overcame him by the blood of the Lamb, and by the word of their testimony...... "

                    <u>*Revelation 12:11*</u>

Dedicated to:

The Financial Seed Sowers of my life,
because you believed in me,
and what God said about me.

Gayle Manning
Island Flavors

Kevin & Toni Bond
Bonded Music Publishing
Bonded Creations

Jude & Cynthia Paillet
Jireh Catering

Sheadrick & Carol Stevenson

TABLE OF CONTENTS

TABLE OF CONTENTS

FOREWORD

Jacqueline has bared her soul in the book *I Wasn't Born This Way*. The writing is realistic and immediately draws the reader into the world of an individual struggling to become whole in a world where she is a victim from early childhood through adolescence. During the formative years and beyond, Jacqueline's emotional behavior and social parameters were set. She began to accept behavior that assaulted her emotional, physical and psychological well being without protest or question. The further she was led away from Godly parameters, the more she was left uncovered and unprotected, the more she eased into a lifestyle that ran contrary to God's design. She wasn't born that way.

The book *I Wasn't Born This Way* highlights the lack of protection experienced by children of this generation. It shows the importance of caring, nurturing parents and the role they play in training emotionally healthy adults. In contrast to the world's assertion that one's sexual preference is predetermined by genes, Ms. Lamar reveals that she developed her principles and lifestyle as a result of unhealthy experiences she endured as a child.

Children have an expectation of protection that was not provided in the life of the writer. *I Wasn't Born This Way* supports the Christian belief that a spiritually grounded family who nurtures, supports and protects children is essential to produce healthy adults. Jacqueline has come through many painful experiences to emerge victorious in Christ.

I Wasn't Born This Way provides wonderful insight into the life of a victorious Christian who was able to put past experiences behind her with God's help. I recommend this book to anyone who is invested in understanding the deception of emotional abuse and healing those who have experienced the horrors of helplessness.

Bishop Eddie L. Long

ACKNOWLEDGEMENTS

ACKNOWLEDGEMENTS

THANKS!!!!!!!!

Pastor David & Bernadette Mills, thank you for always being there for me, time and time again, even when I moved to Georgia.

Sis. Christine Humphrey, for speaking this book into my life. Over eight years ago, you told me "I had a flare for writing."

Mom & Pop Carrington, for always believing in me. Always being my number one fans! Pop thank you for teaching me to let the man walk on the "curb side" of the street, for always "opening my door" and "pulling out my chair."

Aunt Dee, for introducing me to a third person called Holy Spirit and for challenging me many times in the process called "YIELDING."

Gayle Manning, for your timeless effort in proofreading and editing to make sure that what God had ordained for me to write was presented in a manner representative of Him.

My Mother, if it had not been for the things that I had been through, I wouldn't have had anything to write about. Thank you for not "aborting" the seed and giving me life even when you were not sure how to develop the seed.

Elder Ernest Kimble, for watering the seed, nurturing the growth of the seed by watching me grow; protecting the harvest of the seed from attacks of parasites, stray animals and the like; for believing in the product that was going to be harvested from the full grown seed.

Bishop Eddie L. Long, Priest of our house, Spiritual Father, Protector, Encourager, and Motivator, for speaking life into my "life". For planting the seed through all of your timely words of impartation; year-in and year-out.

And most of all I thank my Heavenly Father, King, Wonderful Counselor, Deliverer, Comforter, Healer, MY GOD for the increase of the seed.

INTRODUCTION

INTRODUCTION

We have been bombarded by the media with legislation and marches for Gay Rights and the right to your own choice in sexual orientation. "I was born this way; I'm not hurting anyone; It's my choice; God gave me these feelings, it must be o.k." In all forms of media, you will hear these statements reverberating through the walls of your mind.

This book touches, I believe, the pulse of the nation and the world. It affects both the believer and the unbeliever alike. The believer says, "as long as they don't bother me, it's o.k." The unbeliever says, "I was born this way because of a gene imbalance."

Society has presented this immoral lifestyle as an accepted one and the Church is expected to embrace it with open, loving arms. We are told to turn our heads and change with the times. More than ever, I believe God is looking for a voice that will challenge the world, and I believe that I am that voice. My voice had been captured and trapped by a homosexual lifestyle, but it has been set free and I am willing to come against what the world says and stand on what God says. My voice will no longer be silent on this issue.

I do not regret my past for it has been a catalyst for my future. Had I not gone through the various circumstances that encompass my life, there would be no destiny and ministry today. I could not be an effective witness to a suicidal victim, had I not experienced suicidal attempts as well as tendencies. I could not reach and snatch homosexuals out of the pit, had I not ever been in that very same pit. I could not share the devastation of being in debt, had I not loss control of my finances. I could not encourage one to *fight*, had I not won a battle myself. I have come to realize that my past failures were a doorway to God's *"Hall of Fame."* My mess has become my message.

Our childhood dictates our future - how we will function as an adult - how we will build relationships - how we will cope with circumstances in life - how we will grow spiritually. I am a firm believer that you are a product of your environment, be it good or bad. But, you don't have to remain that product. You can become new and improved. As my dear friend Bernadette once told me, "you now have a new marketing agent, Jesus." II Corinthians 5:17 says, *"Therefore if any man be in Christ, he is a new [creation]; old things are passed away; behold all things are become new."*

As a child, I loved wearing my hair in ponytails and on special occasions, curls; wearing ribbons, frilly dresses and patent leather shoes. But something happened that changed my orientation. *It was not how I was born, but what I would learn.*

I will examine some of the behavior patterns in my environment that attributed to my pursuing the homosexual lifestyle. This lifestyle destroys spiritually through the hardening of the heart to the Word and the ways of God. It destroys mentally through depression and suicidal tendencies, and physically through suicide, murder, and the rise of sexually transmitted diseases. And, of course, through the AIDS epidemic.

According to God's Word, our sexual orientation has been settled before the foundations of the world, long before our mother and father conceived us. The goal of this book is to present to the Parent a guide on raising spiritually confident, and emotionally secure children who have had a strong foundation of love and affirmation laid out for them. It will teach parents to look out for signs of upcoming problems. For Teens it will be a guide that will warn them of impending destruction if they are dabbling in pornography, the occult, homosexuality or any immoral behavior. Now is the time to seek help, while there is chance! To the Homosexual this will be a guide to the Word of God and what God says about the lifestyle and the consequences of the lifestyle. Change is possible, and there is hope for deliverance. There is one hope and one way out, the *full surrender* of one's life to Jesus Christ.

Perhaps my message will be a forewarning and will rescue other victims. We'll look at those actions which gave birth to this debilitating lifestyle; a lifestyle for which *I was not born into*, nor is anyone else.

CULTIVATION

CULTIVATION

Cultivate

In agriculture, cultivation of a particular soil is very important. It determines what crops are best harvested from it. Irrigation is a main factor as well; certain crops require more water than others. You certainly would not want to plant wheat and barley in an area that has never-ending rainfalls.

The fields or grounds must be plowed and the soil fertilized in preparation for sowing of the seeds. Also, the fields must be secured against injury or destruction from wild animals by hedges, fences, or walls. An improper process in cultivation could result in a disaster at harvest time.

As a parent, you must make sure that your child's environment in which he or she is going to be raised has been cultivated, prepared, and secured against the many evils that will come against him or her.

My childhood was not a secure one. Many *wild animals* began to invade my fields. The fields of my life had not been properly protected.

Deuteronomy 6:6-9 - *"And these words, which I command thee this day, shall be in thine heart; And thou shalt teach them diligently unto thy children, and shalt talk of them when thou sittest in thine house, and when thou walkest by the way, and when thou liest down, and when thou risest up. And thou shalt bind them for a sign upon thine hand, and they shall be as frontlets between thine eyes. And thou shalt write them upon the posts of thy house, and on thy gates."*

My mother was a single parent. She was a nurse and worked many different shifts leaving me home often with my brother. At this time about 1966, I was about age 7 and my brother was about age 16. I do thank the Lord that he never once took advantage of me; I never had to worry about the cruel act of incest. My brother protected me, and always took pride in saying that I was his baby sister.

My brother was in high school so he would be gone all day. For some months, my mother was able to secure a baby-sitter for me. I would go to the baby-sitter for lunch; by the time school was out my brother was home. My babysitters were an older couple whose children were grown and had moved away from home, they now had grandchildren. This only lasted for a short while for one of their children had taken sick and one thing had led to the other.

However, it was just long enough for me to encounter my first of many perverted sexual experiences. I remember it so vividly. Their grandson (I'll call him Harry) would come over for lunch on some days as well. I loved to eat lunch there, she served the best lunches. My snack would always be a glazed donut (fresh from the Bond Bakery that was located on Market Street and she would always serve me Campbell's Tomato Soup - one of my favorites).

Here you have two children curious about their development, sexuality, and each other's body parts. I would look at the sales advertisements in the newspaper and point to the body parts of the woman in the advertisement that I wanted Harry to touch; he would do the same. This went on for many days.

One day during lunch we tiptoed upstairs. We were not allowed to go upstairs for anything except to go to the bathroom. However, that's the excuse we used when Harry's grandmother asked where we were. We stood in the back room and he showed me his "penis." I touched it and it was wet and little. That was the first time that I even knew what a penis was or that's what a boy had. You see, things like that were taboo in my house, even when it should have been discussed it was not. You see, I learned "everything that I wanted to know about sex and the body, but was afraid to ask," on the corner, and during recess and lunch time in the school yard. Sad commentary! Needless to say most of the information that I got was perverted and erroneous.

Soon after that encounter with Harry, he stopped coming over for lunch and soon my babysitting services were stopped. It was time to be a latch-key kid.

Child cultivation will also involve the forethought of a parent knowing the great potential of the product (child) that was produced. A parent must speak destiny and direction into their child or children. A parent must realize that a child is the greatest gift one will receive, for that gift will have a lasting impact, possibly on the world.

A CHILD LEFT TO HIMSELF

A CHILD LEFT TO HIMSELF

Irrigate

The farmer cannot just prepare the fields for cultivation and leave it unattended. He has to see that the irrigation system is functioning properly; that the water holes are not clogged with debris. He has to make sure that no wild animals, rodents or insects have taken residence in the soil.

"...A child left to himself bringeth his mother to shame."-
Proverbs 29:15

Too much time left alone for a child can be the most *deadly* thing.

I spent a lot of time alone. I played by myself and talked to myself. I even conjured up an *imaginary friend*. You might say, "well, I've had one of those too, so what's wrong with an imaginary friend?"

I'll tell you, I began to use my imaginary friend as someone to pass the blame and guilt to. Dwelling in the pretend world is a dangerous tool that allows you to escape reality. The problem is if you stay there too long, you won't want to come back. Many mental patients are trapped in a world all their own that they have escaped to.

I drifted into many uncharted waters during my times alone. Uncharted waters such as *pornography* and the *occult*.

Too many children today are being left alone, entertaining themselves and not being properly supervised. On April 20, 1999, our nation experienced the aftermath of one of the deadliest school shootings in U.S. history. Two teenagers who spent too much time alone planned the vengeful shootings at Columbine High School in Littleton, Colorado.

Who's playing with your child?

As I progressed to teenage years, my mother would buy me board games for Christmas. Why? I don't know. I had no one to play them with and she certainly took no time out to play them with me.

I resorted to a lot of reading. "Good",... one might say - but it all depended upon the type of reading I was doing. Oftentimes my reading was of the pornographic nature and material dealing with things of the occult.

The *"Eight Ball"* - a round black ball that was filled with some sort of liquid with a dial in it which had numbers and the words - yes, no, and maybe print-ed on the dial, was one such game. You would ask it a question and you'd wait for the answer to appear in the eight ball's window.

The big brother to the eight ball was the *"Ouija Board."* This is a popular game often played at sleepovers, or in the basement of someone's home with very little lighting or the lights out completely. The atmosphere is now set. *The Dictionary of Mysticism* defines the Ouija board as follows:

> An instrument for communication with the spirits of the dead. Made in various shapes and designs, some of them used in the sixth century before Christ. The common fea-ture of all its varieties is that an object moves under the hand of the medium, and one of its corners, or a pointer attached to it, spells out messages by successively pointing to letters of the alphabet marked on a board which is a part of the instrument (Frank Gaynor, ed., *Dictionary of Mysticism*, New York: Citadel Press, n.d., p. 132).

I became exposed as a teenager to the *psychic world*, through the vehicle of Astrology. I would have to know what my *horoscope* said before I got too far into the day.

"Astrology" is an ancient practice that assumes that the stars and planets have a direct influence upon people and events. Supposedly, one's life pattern can be charted by determining the position of the stars and planets at the time of one's birth. The chart that attempts to accomplish this is known as a "horo-scope" (Josh McDowell & Don Stewart, *Understanding the Occult*, San Bernardino, CA: Here's Life Publishers, Inc., 1982, p. 25).

A common pick-up line in the seventies was "What's your sign?" referring to the Zodiac signs (Capricorn, Libra, Leo, etc.). The name of your sign was associated with the month of your birth, January, February, March, etc.

As a youth (and continuing into young adulthood), I allowed many *super-stitions* to dictate my decisions. These include: *Friday 13th* - nothing major would be planned on this date. *Breaking a mirror* would bring seven years of bad luck. (Do you know that right about now my life today should be destroyed, because of all the mirrors I broke, accidentally as well as intentionally). And there were others: Splitting the pole, the black cat crossing in front of you at night, walking under a ladder, stepping on a colony of ants, stepping on a crack in the sidewalk (if you stepped on a crack, you could break your mother's back) and if you knocked over the salt shaker, you had to throw salt over one of your shoulders. These are just to name a few of the demonic suggestions and influences that began to take charge of my life from childhood.

Parents take note of the many deaths that are occurring around our nation involving the occult, particularly in the late 90's. Teens are now involved in witchcraft, séances, and the offering up of objects and animals, as well as people, as sacrifice to demon gods.

On October 28, 1997, the television show Dateline NBC aired a segment involving teenagers nationwide in satanic worship and ritual practices. Pearl High School in Pearl, Mississippi was not exempt from the diabolical behavior of teens. Six teenagers would be charged with murder. It was later found that the murders involved satanic rituals and practices. A shooting rampage ended the lives of two fellow students and a student's mother. One of the teens involved (Luke Woodham, age 16 who was the ring leader) used a hunting rifle. Practices such as the sacrificing of cats, dogs, goats and the drinking of blood were common in this little town of Mississippi. Other towns, such as West Memphis Arkansas in 1993 lost three young boys. Their deaths were attributed to satanic worship. Television and video games are responsible for fueling much of the interest in the occult.

In the next few paragraphs of this chapter, I plan to present some television shows of the past and present that subtly introduced the occult world to viewers covertly or openly.

Bewitched

There is nothing innocent about this show. At an early age, I had been exposed to the occult through the viewing of this particular program, which was quite blatant in its occult practices. There were three types of characters portrayed on Bewitched, the witches, the warlocks and the mortals.

Mind you, there were and still are many other programs that are filled with occult practices, such as the Frankenstein and Vampire films, etc. I chose Bewitched because it was subtle and tried to use comedy to camouflage the evil intent of this show, that of witchcraft.

Darrin obviously did not check out Samatha's family lineage during their courtship. If he had, he would have found out from the onset that she came from a family of witches and warlocks. Darrin tried to be the man of the house, however, if Sam didn't like his decision she could blink him into a "tadpole" or make him "pint size."

Endora was Samantha's mother. Incidentally, the town of Endor is the place Saul traveled to consult a witch that dwelled there (I Samuel 28:7-25). Endor is a town with many coves in the hillside, a fit dwelling place for mediums and such. Endora despised Darrin and often turned him into one thing or another to get him out of the way of things the family was planning. The other family members who were witches included Tabitha (Sam and Darrin's daughter), Aunt Isadora, Aunt Hagatha and Aunt Esmeralda (the nutty witches), Aunt Clara and Serena (the cousin). The warlock members of the family included Uncle Arthur (the practical joker), Maurice (Sam's father who did not like Darrin), and Adam (Sam and Darrin's son). Darrin, the mortal never had a chance, he was surrounded by evil.

Now for your viewing pleasures there is "Sabrina The Teenage Witch", "Buffy The Vampire Slayer," "Charmed" and "Smallville" all saturated in occult practices. And let us not forget about the series of Friday the 13th movies, all of which were box office hits. There are just too many to name.

Dark Shadows

The title alone indicates darkness and evil. The show was a long running, bone chilling horror that exalted the unknown, ghosts, vampires, and the psychic world. It was much like a soap opera without the sex; each day's episode would be interrupted at the point of a vampire's bite or the hairs beginning to appear on the arms and neck of a man. The werewolves, vampires, ghosts, coffins, wooden stakes, and shrilling screams were the climactic ending of each show.

Walt Disney, The World of Disney, The Disney Show

(Disney! Yes, Disney!) In viewing Disney movies and films, you have to be very prayerful and selective. Many of Disney movies and films are laced with the occult - witchcraft, wizards, sorcerers, magic (spells, charms, and potions) black magic, enchanters, hypnotism, ghosts, and fortune telling (palm reading, tarot card reading, crystal ball reading). Also strong suggestions of the New Age - channeling, invoking of spirits, chanting, scenes that are designed to deal with the *inner force*.

And while I'm on the subject of Walt Disney Co., it is a corporation that is in full support of the gay rights movement.

Some of the old western movies and films often showed individuals dowsing. "***Dowsing***" is the search for and location of underground springs and other objects beneath the ground by the use of a divining rod. The divining rod is a v-shaped wooden twig or piece of wire from six to eighteen inches in length, which is used by the dowser, the person who possesses this ability to search for underground objects. The rod is held firmly in the hands of the dowser until the force coming from the underground object causes the rod to snap over." (Josh McDowell & Don Stewart, *Understanding the Occult*, San Bernardino, CA: Here's Life Publishers, Inc., 1982, p. 63).

Witchcraft is forbidden:

Exodus 22:18 - *"Thou shalt not suffer a witch to live."*

Leviticus 19:26b - *"Do not practice divination or sorcery."* (NIV)

Leviticus 19:31 - *"Regard not them that have familiar spirits, neither seek after wizards, to be defiled by them; I am the Lord your God."*

Deuteronomy 18:9-12 - *"When thou art come into the land which the Lord thy God giveth thee, thou shalt not learn to do after the abominations of those nations. There shall not be found among you anyone who maketh his son or his daughter pass through the fire, or who useth divination, or an observer of times, or an enchanter, or a witch, Or a charmer, or a consulter of [mediums], or a wizard, or a **necromancer***. For all that do these things are an abomination unto the Lord; and because of these abominations the Lord thy God doth drive them out from before thee."*

*A **necromancer** is one who attempts to conjure up the spirits of the dead for purposes of magically revealing the future or influencing the course of events.

> **Galatians 5:19a-21** - *"Now the works of the flesh are manifest, which are these: ... Idolatry, [sorcery], hatred, [strife], [jealousy], wrath, [factions], seditions, heresies, envyings, murders, drunkenness, revelings, and the like; of which I tell you before, as I have also told you in time past, that they who do such things shall not inherit the kingdom of God."*

This next television show leaves a few questionable practices in the viewers mind.

"In the House"

The character Marion (played by L. L. Cool J) was an ex-football player who moved into a room over his garage and rented out his house to boarders to bring in extra income. The character Jackie (played by Debbie Allen) after a bitter divorce left her husband, rented the house, and moved in with her two children.

Now, explain this one to me. You and your teenage daughter move into a house with a well-stacked ex-foot-ball player - I mean *buffed* and you don't even know the man? That is not a wise decision.

The character Tiffany (the teenage daughter) is manipulative. She is always managing to persuade her mother into letting her do certain things, oftentimes lying to get permission. The character is written so that she is portrayed as somewhat of an airhead. One who does not make good decisions, although I know where she got that from.

The character Austin (the son) is an eight year old who wears glasses and is underdeveloped. He is longing for some male bonding and mentoring. He misses his father, therefore, he makes it very easy for Marion to be any kind of influence on him. There was one episode in which Austin just wanted to be accepted by his peers. He had taken note that Marion was the *player* amongst the women and always had friends, especially female friends around. So Austin went to school dressed like Marion (hat turned backwards, pants hanging off his behind, and one of his pants legs rolled up); that impressed the girls as well as the boys in his class. But he could not continue this charade because in order to be cool, he had to take his glasses off and he could not quite see without them.

> **Joshua 24:14-15** - *"Now, therefore, fear the Lord, and serve him in sincerity and in truth; and put away the gods which your fathers served on the other side of the [river], and in Egypt, and serve ye the Lord. And if it seem evil unto you to serve the Lord, choose you this day whom ye will serve, whether the gods which your fathers served that were on the other side of the [river], or the gods of the Amorites, in whose land ye dwell; but as for me and my house, we will serve the Lord."*

The show's leading character (Marion) is portrayed as a Buddhist and on many episodes the practices have been clearly addressed (the Buddha statue, meditation, etc.). He has often made statements about being, *"one with the universe," "being in harmony," "your spirituality,"* and *"your karma."* The practices he refers to are that of Nichiren Shoshu Buddhism, its founder was Nichiren Daishonin (A.D. 1222 - 1282).

According to the Christian Research Institute Journal, some recording stars and many hundreds of thousand of other Americans, are followers of Nichiren Shoshu Buddhism (NS), (John Weldon, *"Nichiren Shoshu Buddhism - Mystical Materialism for the Masses,"* Christian Research Institute Journal, Fall 1992, p8).

In an article written by William M. Alnor, he stated that NS is among the most influential of the new religions that have come on the scene in recent decades. The movement claims 17 million members in over 117 countries (William M. Alnor, *"Name It and Claim It Style of Buddhism Called America's Fastest Growing Religion,"* *Christian Research Journal*, Winter/ Spring 1989, p 26).

A television show that practices and displays a religion that believes that God is dead and that the doctrine of creation is foolish and childish, certainly does not warrant my viewing. Psalms 14:1 - *"The fool hath said in his heart, there is no God. They are corrupt, they have done abominable works, there is none that doeth good."*

Star Trek
For all of you devoted fans, known as *"Trekkies"* or *"Trekkers,"* Star Trek has a lot to say about God, humanity, war, sex, ethics, and the like. The creator of Star Trek, Gene Roddenberry, rejected Christianity as a young teen

because it seemed to him to be nonsense. After producing Star Trek, he developed a conscious philosophy and sought to communicate it in his work, that philosophy is know as *Humanism*.

Writer Robert M. Bowman, Jr. of the Christian Research Institute Journal says about Star Trek, "There is an implication that belief in God is unnecessary." In one episode, *"The Tholian Web,"* where Captain Kirk is rescued from a parallel universe through Spock's skillful use of the *"transporter"* (a device used to transport people and objects immediately from the ship to other locations or the reverse), Chief Engineer Montgomery Scott ("Scotty") exclaims, "Thank heaven!" But Spock protests that "there was no deity involved - it was my cross circuiting to "B" that brought the Captain back!" When Chief Medical Officer Leonard "Bones" McCoy responds, "Thank pitchforks and pointy ears, as long as it worked," Kirk agrees: "That's a fair statement, Bones."

The humanistic philosophy of Star Trek, while it rejects the supernatural God of Christianity, is not aridly atheistic. It is rather, a religious humanism, a cosmic faith in humanity. This is obvious in Star Trek V: The Final Frontier. Sybok's "God" is revealed to be a devilish entity. McCoy wonders if God is really "out there" somewhere in the universe. Kirk's answer: Maybe God is not out there, but is "in the human heart." (Is God not in the Vulcan heart, too?)

Star Trek is best known for its Vulcans, Klingons, Romulans, and other extraterrestrials. There is the assumption that humanity owes its existence to evolution rather than creation. (Robert M. Bowman, Jr., *"Strange New Worlds: The Humanist Philosophy of Star Trek," Christian Research Journal*, Fall 1991, p. 20).

All of the television shows named and many others are leaving our children, teens and adults open to the influences of Satan and the Satanic world.

The following paragraphs describe a subtle practice being instituted in many corporations, organizations, and small businesses and even in our public and private educational systems. That practice is known as a "Stress Management Program." Other disguises are Biofeedback, Creative Visualization, and many others under the New Age teaching.

As a young adult, I would also be thrust into New Age and Eastern Mysticism practices such as trance channeling through *meditation* practices, or sometimes noted under the disguise of relaxation and yoga techniques. Many businesses are using these practices to help their employees' cope with work related stress, as well as the personal stress oftentimes brought on by their positions.

In the early ninety's, I was working for a paralegal agency. These techniques were presented as a Stress Management Program offered by the employer. It was mandatory that each employee attended these sessions sponsored by the employer. The sessions consisted of a large room with chairs positioned in a circle, and a *coach* or *guide* who would instruct us as to what to do.

The episode began with everyone getting as comfortable as possible, some lying on the floor, others sitting in a chair, and some leaning against a wall. The purpose or intent of the guide was to teach you to relax and to achieve susceptible states of consciousness. Instrumental music was played, that of birds and waterfalls, sounds of chimes could be heard as well. The guide told us to relax and picture yourself going through this doorway. The guide further told us to walk down this long corridor leaving behind things that caused us stress. The guide told us to reach for the light at the end of the corridor. I began to sink into a deep trance that lasted for over an hour. The guide then instructed us to awake.

It was at that point that I made myself even more vulnerable and opened to the spirit world.

It was a funny thing though, I do remember that prior to this Stress Management Program, the company was doing very well financially. But shortly afterwards, business began to decline. This company had, I believe, experienced one of the consequences of delving into the satanic realm.

Because I had been exposed to the level of satanic influences that I had as a child, as an adult it was much easier to accept occult practices and not know the fatal consequences of these practices. Theses practices were now very subtle and I was oblivious to them, they had become a way of life.

Parents make sure friends, family members, babysitters or church folk are mirroring what you as a parent are teaching at home. If not, this is a sure ingredient for a disaster. As a parent, you should mind who you are leaving your children with for supervision, it could become an outer world experience for them. A world for which you nor your child is equipped to handle.

AFFIRMATION, A MATTER OF LIFE OR DEATH

AFFIRMATION: A MATTER OF LIFE OR DEATH

"Who's going to affirm me?"

> **Sowing**
> It is very important to the farmer that he plants the correct seed. If the farmer harvests corn, surely he did not sow an apple seed. The seed has to be sown at an exact time and an exact location in order for the crop to grow. If the seed is sown in an uncultivated area, it will die; areas such as a stony ground, the wayside or among thorns.

Jesus in one of his parables used the seed and soil to illustrate the Word of God in our lives. It is sometimes *sown* improperly, which results in a bad crop or no crop at all.

> **Matthew 13:3-8** - *"And he spoke many things unto them in parables, saying, Behold, a sower went forth to sow; And when he sowed, some of the seeds fell by the wayside, and the fowls came and devoured them. Some fell upon stony places, where they had not much earth; and forthwith they sprang up, because they had no deepness of earth. And when the sun was up, they were scorched; and because they had no root, they withered away. And some fell among thorns; and the thorns sprang up, and choked them. But other seeds fell into good ground, and brought forth fruit, some an hundredfold, some sixtyfold, some thirtyfold."*

As with the farmer, it should be very important to a parent what is sown into a child's beginning seed time. As a child, many of the wrong seeds were sown into my life, which resulted in a *bad harvest* in later years. Seeds of tension, anger, verbal abuse and sexual abuse were sown at an early age.

In the late 1980s, a former pastor of mine, from Pennsylvania, did a sermon that dealt with some root issues of homosexuality. There are some environmental traits that are common in individuals who have <u>chosen</u> the lifestyle. A domineering mother, a passive father, an alcoholic mother or father, an abusive father or mother, an absent father or male presence, lack of affirmation and love.

A few of these traits I could attest to in my life. I'm not saying that if a child experiences these environmental traits he will become a homosexual, but I am saying that if you would ask a majority of the homosexual community about their upbringing you would find that one, two, or more of these traits existed.

One thing I can be sure of though is that any of these environmental traits in any child's upbringing will result in trouble if not dealt with early.

Speak Life!

Children need constant affirmation - speak to your child. They can understand you. Tell them:

"You are special."
"I couldn't wait to hold you today."
"I'm glad you were born."
"What would I do without you."
"You make my day."
"I think about you all day at work."

And mean it! Children can detect a *sarcastic* or *patronizing* spirit, they also can detect a *sincere* one. They are able to sense whether you mean something or not.

A touch should accompany these words of affirmation. As a child if I had been touched more by my mother, other than a *beating*, I would not have had to go elsewhere to get that touch.

Or Speak Death!

Statements like these should be avoided:

"Can't you do anything right?"
"Why are you so bad?"
"You make me sick."
"Don't be so stupid."
"Shut-up!"
"You're just like your..."

"Why can't you be like…?"

The most disturbing part is that some of you who are reading this book will have read books over and over again about positive affirmation, and you will still say the same destructive words to your child.

Highway and public transportation billboards display *"Words Hurt,"* but parents continue to allow destructive words to spew from their mouths in fits of anger and rage. <u>Proverbs 18:21a</u> - *"Death and life are in the power of the tongue…"*

There is an old adage *"sticks and stones may break my bones but words will never hurt me."* Quite frankly, I'd rather have had my mother break a few of my bones then say some of the things she said to me as a child. Bones do eventually heal, however, a broken and wounded spirit takes much longer to heal, if it ever heals. A wounded spirit is a painful thing to endure. You always feel the pain of old words.

<u>Proverbs 18:14</u> - *"The spirit of a man will sustain his infirmity; but a wounded spirit, who can bear?"*

Think about the emotional security that you longed for from a friend, husband, wife, mother, father, or relative. That's the same emotional security that a child longs for. God designed us for fellowship. When you don't receive it, you *die* emotionally.

I was not affirmed as a child. There was no *"That-a-girl, I knew you could do it, I had faith in you, You make me proud, or I'm glad you were born."* Not receiving affirmation made me very competitive in nature and I wanted to prove to all who I encountered that I could do it even though others thought I couldn't. I did not want to lose. I began to equate how much a person loved me with how well I did something. If I failed, you hated me. If I did well, I had the chance of being loved.

When a child receives affirmation and affection from home, that child will not have to look outside of the home to receive those needs.

But let me state firmly, *"I know who I am in Christ now, it is a liberating thing too."* *"I am accepted in the beloved,"* <u>Ephesians 1:6</u>. This was one of the hardest principles for me to learn. I was always so used to trying to prove something to people and trying to be accepted.

Who am I?

I was born on January 9, 1959, and raised in Philadelphia, Pennsylvania. I was never told anything much about my birth, other than I was born the same night Aunt Jane died. What a thing to tell a child. For years I thought that my being born was predicated on Aunt Jane dying. I didn't even know my Father's name until I was in my 20's. That issue was kept hush-hush. It kept me asking a lot of questions in my early teens, that were ignored most of the time, or the conversation was quickly changed to another subject.

It was rough not having an *identity,* not knowing who I was, who brought me here. Was I wanted? Was I a mistake? Did my parents want to keep me? I have always felt that I was a *"passion child,"* conceived in a heated moment of passion, a one-night stand. When my brother was angry he used to tell me that my father was no good, neither was his.

One day when I was home alone, (one of many times) I was going through some of my mothers belongings (probing as my grandmother often called it). I found inside of a dresser drawer, a slide of a man that I believe could have been my father. He appeared to be tall, carmel-colored, with curly black hair. (Do any of you men out there fit that description, and had a child out of wedlock forty-four years ago that you would like to claim? I'm house broken!) Oh, and by the way, you are long overdue on your child support!

During my pre-adolescent years I really longed for a father in my life. Those were the times I needed a male figure, someone that I could call *dad*. Someone to affirm that I'm his *girl*, that "no matter if you do good or not, I'm going to love you."

The story told to me was that my father died before I was born, of colon cancer. Did I believe the story - NO! I've been around too many young ladies who were burnt by men and became bitter from a one-night-stand that left them pregnant and alone to raise a child. Rather than tell the child their mistake, they tell the child the father is dead or lives overseas. I felt that I was just another one of those statistics.

When I was in my twenties, I met a woman who I was told was my father's sister. The visit was cold and unattached; not much conversation took place. Surprisingly, my mother initiated the visit. It still left me with a lot of questions that went unanswered. What do you say to someone you have never met and they've never met you in twenty plus years? ("Hey Auntie, you've missed my last twenty something birthdays.") As I write this book, I can't even think of her name. I do remember that she owned a Barber Shop called "Larry's." I believe that was my father's name. It was a one-time visit. I believe my mother had talked to her on several occasions since then. The last I heard about her was that she was sick. That had been some years ago.

I grew up with no male presence, no man to speak into my life. As a result, when I got older, I looked for it in any man. It would further result in my being in bad hetero-relationships when I began to date.

Today, however, it no longer matters who my father is or was. I have come to realize over the years that my father was only able to disburse the seed that produced me, but he was not capable of fathering me. I have sought and found solace in my heavenly Father. He has proven once at Calvary that I'm his child and of the love He has for me. He has proven over and over again that He cares for me and is concerned about what concerns me. He has proven to be the perfect example of a man. He is my provider and protector.

A father's presence is crucial for the development of a male or female child. My pastor, Bishop Eddie L. Long, shared in a message on Sunday, May 18, 1997, entitled "*Back to the Future*," the importance of the male authority and presence in the home. He stated, "a father brings out the femininity of the daughter and the masculinity of the son."

When a father is giving his daughter affirmation as a girl, telling her how special she is to him, she won't fall for some line a guy gives her. She will already have been told how beautiful and special she is. So now *home boy* will have to come with something better.

When a father speaks into his son of the potential that's in him and how he can conquer the odds, the son will aspire to be the best. He will not run from a challenging situation, because his father told him that he could do whatever God has called him to do; because God has given him the power to accomplish the task or assignment. A father must teach his son how to love his mother, sister, or any woman. But dads, first make sure that you are loving your wife, or any woman you are associated with as well. This will teach your sons to look for a particular young lady when seeking a wife, and also how to respect women.

Joseph's example!

In Genesis 37:3, it clearly stated that Jacob loved Joseph more than all his children, because he was the son of his old age. (Boy, talk about favoritism.) That meant he gave more affirmation and attention to Joseph, giving him special things, such as the *coat of many colors*. I must admit I probably would have tried to bump my sister off too knowing that my mother had a greater love for her than me. I imagine that a lot of Jacob's attention was given to Joseph and his other brothers felt the rejection and isolation. They died emotionally and they wanted to kill the very one who was luring emotional life away from them.

I love you just the way you are!

As a pre-teen, I had somewhat of a height problem. I was physically challenged - O.K. I was tall, thin and nothing fit me. My pants always showed my socks - O.K. I wore highwaters - ready for a flood at any time. Many times my classmates would ridicule me and I would run home in tears, but my mother was not there for me to share my humiliation. Children then, as well as now, can be verbally abusive towards their peers.

Today's society places such emphasis on your dress. I'm glad that some public schools have adopted the uniform code.

The ridicule about my dress resulted in a complex about my size. I usually always ended up in the back of the school yard line, classroom, or cafeteria line. You name it and I was in back of that line. To top it off, I had skinny legs. My peers called me "stilt, twiggy, tree, bony, and string bean." As a child struggling with who I was, these nick names further compounded my identity crisis.

To add insult to injury, I had no breasts (not little), but no breasts. My mother was not equipped to encourage me to know that regardless of how I looked, she still loved me. As I think about this, my mother was pretty much built the same way. I wonder, did she have the same complex about her body as well?

I did not know that I had been *"fearfully and wonderfully made"* - Psalms 139:14. Neither did I know that height had its advantages. I did not have to stand on a stool - the best position in basketball was yours, if you could play. Modeling agents had great demand for the tall and the thin.

"I had to come to the realization that God made me the way he did for a purpose, not as some cruel joke."

For the last twenty years, thin is in! Just look at the weight loss industry, how they have capitalized on people who are *weight challenged*. The industry, by the way, has made billions in profit annually. Now some of the diet pills (phen-fen) that are on the market have been recalled because of hazardous ingredients.

Look at the masses of people that have paid Jenny Craig, Weight Watchers, Richard Simmons and all of the other weight loss professionals their money only to tip the scale when problems and issues arise in their lives.

I bet if the truth were told, somebody called them "fatty, porky, two-tons-of-fun, tubby, or piggy." They think that dieting will solve their problems, but there is an inner conflict. They have to deal with some inner issues in order for the diet to be effective. Now I'm not going to blame all weight problems on inner conflict. There are some people who just need some discipline and should stay away from that *quarter pounder*.

As a teenager I was withdrawn, sensitive and my *spirit* had already been broken and wounded as a child. Some of the things that my mother had said to me as a child left such a stigma on me.

I grew up in a family that was not one for giving encouraging words. We had a way of *sounding off* or *bussing*, as we called it, on people. We were often cruel and critical towards one another.

We said things that might have sounded funny but surely they were not edifying to the hearers. That habit has stayed with me through the years and the Lord is still breaking me from it. It was not a healthy environment for building character or self-esteem. Hurting words from my mother and some family members left me with *damaged emotions* that the Lord has healed with his love that drew me from the pit that the destructive words had driven me into.

The home is where most youth's problems will begin. The negative things that are said to them as children will result in problems in later years. They are looking for affirmation and seek to get it from whomever or whatever gives it to them. That is how they are drawn, like butterflies to a flower or bees to a honeycomb.

Parents, the next time that you are tempted to say something destroying to your child - don't!

Affirmation is a matter of life or death!

THE POWER OF A TOUCH

THE POWER OF A TOUCH

Nurturing

Any person who grows plants soon will learn that touching is a vital part of the growth of their plants. Now some people go as far as talking and singing to them. I will pop a *praise tape* in for them. I have found that to be very effective.

Touch (Webster's Dictionary) - to bring a bodily part into contact with, especially so as to perceive through the tactile sense; handle or feel gently usually with the intent to understand or appreciate; to lay hands upon with intent to heal; to have an influence on: affect; to leave a mark or impression on; to have a bearing: relate on or upon; to move to sympathetic feeling; to strike or push lightly; to commit violence upon; to put hands upon in any way or degree; to harm slightly by or as if by contact: taint, blemish; to hurt the feelings of: wound.

The power of a **touch** can offer such a ministry of healing, it also can destroy self-worth, aspirations, hopes and a life.

A **touch** could have grave consequences, the kings were warned -*"Saying touch not mine anointed, and do my prophets no harm."* - I Chronicles 16:22.

Satan wanted God to **touch** all that Job had in hopes that he would curse God and die. Job 1:11 - *"But put forth thine hand now, and touch all that he hath, and he will curse thee to thy face."*

The woman with the issue of blood felt that a **touch** was so important, that she only wanted to **touch** the "hem" of Jesus' garment. Matthew 9:20-21 - *"And, behold, a woman, who had been diseased with an issue of blood* *twelve years, came behind him, and touched the hem of his garment; For she said within herself, If I may but touch his garment, I shall be [well]."*

Jesus' **touch** was so powerful that human saliva (spit) became medicinal. Mark 8:22-25 - *"And he cometh to Bethsaida; and they bring a blind man unto him, and besought him to touch him. And he took the blind man by the hand, and led him out of the town; and when he had spit on his eyes, and put his hands upon him, he asked him if he saw [anything]. And he looked up, and said, I see men like trees, walking. After that he put his hands again upon his eyes, and made him look up; and he was restored, and saw every man clearly."*

A **touch** meant so much to Jesus that he rebuked his disciples when they hindered the children from coming. Mark 10:13-14 - *"And they brought young children to him, that he should touch them; and his disciples rebuked those that brought them. But when Jesus saw it, he was much displeased, and said unto them, [permit] the little children to come unto me, and forbid them not; for of such is the kingdom of God."*

A **touch** by a man could arouse a woman, and especially if she is not married to him. Paul warned men, don't do it. I Corinthians 7:1 - *"Now concerning the things about which ye wrote unto me, it is good for a man not to touch a woman."*

Pass the peace

In my fellowship there is a segment of our service called *"pass the peace."* At this juncture of the service we embrace other people with hugs sitting around us. Sometimes it may have been the only hug someone received that day or week. It's a healing time for many.

Although I like to be hugged, when I first came to New Birth in 1996, I was still learning how to give a hug more willingly, or under less restraint. At times I was very uncomfortable with hugging. I did not have a problem hugging people I knew. It was the ones I did not know. After being abused, you learn to evaluate a hug.

There is one sister in our church, who gives the greatest hugs. When I first started getting established in my church, I always looked forward to receiving hugs from her. They are warm and nurturing.

On the other hand, there were a couple of brothers who come to mind, when they hugged me, I felt like an octopus was attacking me. They were all arms. One guy in particular after he has kissed you he leaves your neck wet.

Needless to say, as the months went by, he only got a wave or a distant hug, very, very brief. It is sad when men as well as women, use this as an opportunity to get their free feel.

Initially, I was very uncomfortable with this process; which stemmed from childhood abuse, it was foreign to me. However, after weeks and weeks of doing this, I began to be freed up.

Most of my generation was exempt from being touched by their parents, relatives, or friends in a positive way. If the truth were told, many of my peers were touched the wrong way. And some still carry the burden of guilt today.

My family was not for touching or hugging (except maybe on holidays). When I was exposed to touching and hugging, I thought that it was foreign and it was very hard to receive. During those years of abuse when I began receiving lots of hugs and touching, it was hard to discern a *good touch* and a *bad touch*.

Children of all ages and walks of life will always welcome healing hands, not hurting hands.

For people you see with problems, hurts, and pain,
were not born that way.
Touch that life and I'll guarantee you,
you will touch their day.
Touch a life and you've touched the world!
Jacqueline Lamar – November, 1997

TRAPPED

TRAPPED

> ## Pruning
>
> In the horticultural world of plant growing, there is a very popular plant called the *Pothos*. There are various species of the Pothos, but one in particular is the *Golden Pothos,* it's the fastest growing plant of the species. It grows vine-like and will begin to wrap around anything near it. It must be monitored on occasion to see if it has wrapped itself around anything and if so, it must be unwrapped, if possible, or cut.

Adolescence is a very impressionable stage in a person's life. How you are handled during this stage in your life can either make or break you, build or destroy you. Constant supervision from parents is a must, if the child is expected to grow without getting trapped into the wrong relationships and wrapped up in the wrong activities.

During this stage of my life it was just my mother and me. By now my brother had left home, by force, not choice. His and my mother's relationship left no strings to mend, it was torn apart by bitterness, rebellion and anger. I would soon follow in the same footsteps. Both my brother and I were trapped by different life circumstances, but nonetheless, we were trapped.

What's that I'm feeling?

I was very curious about my body and the parts that were beginning to develop, as I imagine any child would be. I could not understand why some girl's parts were larger than others.

In about 5th grade, I had a classmate (I'll call her Betty) who was about three or four times my size - we were very curious about one another's body parts. She lived not far from where I did and I would go to her house - she was a latch-key kid as well. We would look at and touch each other's private parts. That was my first time seeing a fully developed girl naked. The touching aroused some feelings, but I was not sure what they were.

After a while, she told some other girls at school and I had the hardest time trying to convince them that Betty was lying. Mind you she wasn't, but how does a nine year old explain that type of sexually illicit behavior?

Down the street from my apartment in the projects lived another set of latch-key kids. My playmate had an older brother. He would take us to his room and fondle us. He would tackle us like he was playing with us and throw us on the bed and lay on us. He would feel too heavy on top of me and I would become frightened and beg for him to get off me. He made us promise not to tell anyone. It was not long before I stopped going to my playmate's house. I was just not feeling comfortable with the game we were playing. I wanted to tell someone, but whom?

By age ten, I was experiencing some feelings from touching, but I was not quite sure what they were. I was enjoying some of the touching. I was a very inquisitive child, always wanting to see how things worked.

Another classmate (I'll call him Tim) often made these feelings surface for me by touching and fondling me during class, in the coatroom and at recess, whenever and wherever I got close to him. This school drama went on for quite some time. One day the drama was taken to an alleyway in the back of a residence where myself and about three or four boys and maybe one other girl, were in the alley fondling one another. It was not until one of the boys leaned against a fence that fell and all the neighborhood dogs began to bark that we ended the after school pre-teen orgy.

I was exposed to pornography at an early age through written material that a classmate's sister wrote. I was in 7th grade and the girl's sister was in 9th. The material was pure "trash" - very explicit in the nature of the sexual acts performed with humans as well as animals. After reading this material it fanned the flames of my heated perversion. We would pass around "XXX" rated books. Just to name one, "Devil in Mrs. Jones" - trust me she had sex with everything, my virgin mind would be exposed to much perversion (at 11 years old). I would keep the material hidden under my bed and sneak to read it. That was the trap that Satan used to get my mind, and believe me he had a strong grip and wouldn't let go. I became "morally polluted."

The pornographic reading material was the trap of my mind that advanced into pornographic movies and videos and later other behaviors. The viewing of pornographic videos and movies would pervert my thoughts and my morals.

By the way, pornography today is a multi-billion dollar industry - *soft core* (picture sexual acts that are not illegal) - *hard core* (picture illegal acts). Pornography consist of *child pornography* (sexual exploitation of a child). Today, sex in advertising is used in every commercial from toothpaste to automobiles, adult videos, dial-a-porn and if things weren't already bad, now we have Internet sex. The bible speaks adamantly on all of these immoral behaviors:

Sexual intercourse outside of marriage - Hebrews 13:4 - *"Marriage is honorable in all, and the bed undefiled, but [fornicators] and adulterers God will judge."*

The law condemned adultery, homosexuality, incest, and bestiality - Leviticus 20:10-23.

The abuse of children - Matthew 18:6 - *"But whosoever shall offend one of these little ones who believe in me, it were better for him that a millstone were hanged about his neck, and that he were drowned in the depth of the sea."*

Foolish talk and filthy jokes - Ephesians 5:3-4 - *"But fornication, and all uncleanness, or covetousness, let it not be once named among you, as becometh saints; Neither filthiness, nor foolish talking, nor jesting, which are not [fitting]; but, rather, giving of thanks."*

Sexual lust - I Corinthians 7:1-2 - *"Now concerning the things about which ye wrote unto me, it is good for a man not to touch a woman. Nevertheless, to avoid fornication, let every man have his own wife, and let every woman have her own husband."* Matthew 5:27-28 - *"Ye have heard that it was said by them of old, Thou shalt not commit adultery; But I say unto you that whosoever looketh on a woman to lust after her hath committed adultery with her already in his heart."*

Vexation of one's spirit man - II Peter 2:7-8 - *"And delivered just Lot, vexed with the filthy [manner of life] of the wicked. (For that righteous man dwelling among them, in seeing and hearing, vexed his righteous soul from day to day with their unlawful deeds)."*

Avoid all evil - II Thessalonians 5:22 - *"Abstain from all appearance of evil."*

New start, same ending

Things had begun to get pretty bad in the projects where we lived. Car burnings, break-ins, gang wars, and stabbings; it was no longer a safe place to live. It was not conducive to raising any child or neither was it an environment that promoted excellence. My mother began looking for other places to live, but being a single parent with one income and a child made it hard to become eligible in other housing situations. It was time to move.

Ironically during this same time my Aunt Ruth was looking for a place to live as well; she wanted to buy a house. When I was in the 10th grade we moved to a house on 56th Street - the radiators leaked, the roof leaked - it just was not a good investment. We stayed there for about a year, if that long. The whole transition for me brought about great anxiety. This was my first year in high school. I could not start high school for two weeks because of the move, that was all that I needed.

After the 56th Street fiasco, my Aunt pursued the purchase of a house on my uncles *GI Bill*. The house was on 59th Street. She lived in it until the day she died. This new house presented a very exciting time for all of us. The house was in a pretty decent neighborhood. We each had our own room, and things looked promising - so I thought. By this stage of the game my *puberty* was in full bloom. I carried an *attitude* the size of Mt. Everest. My emotions were in an uproar and I did not know who I was or whose I was. My aunt and mother did not get along well at all. There was constant bickering and disagreements.

One night my mother and I had an argument about something - we did that often. She never talked to you, she talked at you. It was whatever she said and that was final. I was never supposed to have an opinion. She was always right and you were always wrong; my mother was very authoritative. She had a tendency of not listening to what anyone said.

Needless to say, my listening skills as a teenager and young adult needed much work. In more recent years, that is an area that the Lord is working on. If what you are saying to me sounds like junk or not worth my while to hear, I'll cut you right off!

The argument my mother and I were having had become so fierce that I ran out of the house that night. I didn't go far, I had no money and nowhere to go.

There was a lot of tension in that house and I began to lose respect for both my aunt and mother.

My aunt did the *party scene* and that bugged the heck out of my mother. My mother slept all the time and left dishes in the sink and that bugged the heck out of my aunt. They both had totally different personalities and it showed. We constantly had traffic coming in and out of the house. My aunt would have her *drinking buddies* over on most weekends. And to top it all off she bought a puppy. Now anyone that has trained a puppy knows that the training process is a pain to say the least. They pull things down and tear things up. We never could have clean laundry because the puppy pulled things off the clotheslines. And to further aggravate things the puppy would dispose of his "gravy train" in the basement. Now that was the last straw. I just could not take it and neither could my mother.

With all of the feuding going on around me and not feeling loved, I withdrew into a *shell* keeping to myself, a world of my own. I would come home from school, eat, wash the dishes and go to my room; that is where I would stay until the next day. Very soon, my mother and I would plan to move to another domicile. But not before I would become trapped in another pit.

> *One summer a cousin of mine came to visit. I felt further slighted when my aunt made such a fuss over her - buying her clothes, taking her to lunch, taking her to visit everyone. I wanted that attention and at that time I didn't have it. My cousin and I spent a lot of time talking about boys. During one of our times together she told me that she was going to show me how to do something that was going to drive me crazy - and it did. That would be my first of many experiences in masturbation. Now I had learned another sexually illicit act that would trap my mind further into the realm of pornography. It became my escape into an area that was off limits. It was a way to self-fulfilling sexual pleasures.*

Masturbation is a destroying act, for it takes away from the original plan of God, for sexual fulfillment that has been designed for marriage only (Hebrews 13:4). The sexual arousal that one obtains through masturbation is certainly defiled. <u>*Defile*</u> means to violate the sanctity of, dishonor. In masturbation you dishonor or violate that which God has designed for the marriage bed. Masturbation deadens the senses. It distorts the natural, and becomes the unnatural by utilizing vibrators, massagers and various sex toys. When these items are used to promote sexual arousal and orgasms, the body is conditioned to wanting these items for the artificial pleasure they initiate; the <u>natural intended methods are then disregarded</u> (for the man, the touch of the woman's vagina on his penis, or the caressing of the female's hands - for the female, the insertion of the man's penis into the vagina or the caressing of the man's hands.) Through masturbation, the mind becomes conditioned to believe that the natural intended methods are not necessary and sexual arousal has now become a one-person act.

My aunt in later years would *fuel the flame* as well. She had cable television and would often encourage me to sit and watch the *adult channels* with her. And for those of you that have perused these channels, you know that there is nothing left for the imagination. *I was hooked*! Eventually when I purchased a VCR I would then have *private viewings* to support my immoral habit.

These pornographic videos, movies, and books would arouse many sexual fantasies that I could not control. Therefore I masturbated to relieve the frustration and sexual tension built up from what I saw.

Never let it be said that pornography does not trap the mind, body, and soul. It starts with the mind through reading and viewing, then the body through various acts and then finally the soul that longs for it. Your mind gets wrapped around all the filth that you can get your hands on. And in order for the mind to be released, you have to *cut the source*.

TRAIN UP A CHILD

TRAIN UP A CHILD

> Many plants that grow wild, such as the spider, pothos and the purple passion can be trained to grow bushy or trained to grow vine-like. You have to *pinch* or *prune* the plant in certain spots in order for it to grow in a particular fashion.

In rearing children, they have to be trained a certain way in order to get the best results. If not, you'll have a *wild-growing* child on your hands.

<u>Proverbs 22:6</u> - *"Train up a child in the way he should go and, when he is old, he will not depart* (NIV says *turn - from it)."* The ABS - English Version says - *"Teach children how they should live, and they will remember it all their life."*

Discipline was no ride on a ferris wheel for me. I hated getting a beating (or "whippin" as we called it). My mother used the storing-up method. She would beat you for everything you did. When she would beat you she would sing - "didn't I tell you such and such," hitting and talking, each stroke on rhythm. Don't sing, just beat me and get it over with!

Now don't get me wrong, I'm not against spanking a child, by no means. I'm not an advocate for *time out* either. I support time on the *behind*. Then they can have time out to think about their behavior. However, there has to be a balance during your disciplining: *Love + Rod = Balance.*

My mother was a nurse and worked the night shift during my last few years in elementary school. One evening I was out past my curfew. She sent my brother to look for me. When I got home, I got the beating of my life (one of the many). It was not until I became an adult that I realized why I got that beating. Two minutes of explanation could have spared me of the bitterness I carried all those years. I should have been told at the time of the beating of the dangers of being out on the street at night.

Our prison facilities are bursting with juvenile delinquents who never had their behinds spanked. And the ones that have been spanked have learned from the system to cry child abuse. The worst thing that a child could have learned is the term *child abuse*. An undisciplined child, one that has no boundaries, guidelines or rules is destined to end up in the juvenile courts.

According to the NCJJ (National Center for Juvenile Justice statistics – www.NCJJ.org), youth under the age of 15 accounted for 67% of all juvenile arrests for arson in 1999. In that same year, law enforcement agencies made an estimated 2.5 million arrests of persons under the age of 18. Juveniles were involved in 16% of all Violent Crime Index arrests and 32% of all Property Crime Index arrests in 1999.

The National Center for Education Statistics (www.nces.ed.gov) reported during 1996-97, about 4,000 incidents of rape or other types of sexual battery were cited in our nation's public schools. About 11,000 incidents of physical attacks or fights with weapons and about 190,000 fights or physical attacks not involving weapons also occurred in the same year.

A general consensus of various statistical reports that I've read, concluded that it cost the judicial system in 2001 nearly $46 billion to operate its prisons. And the United States spends on an average of $7,000 or so per year to educate a youth, and over $35,000 to lock up a youth. There is certainly something wrong with this reporting.

The second worst thing for society is the government dipping their noses into areas of discipline that God has ordained for the parents to handle. Now if the government wants to continue paying $35,000 plus per year to house a felon, then keep sticking its nose into God's business, and forcing parents to relinquish their God-given rights, there won't be a budget large enough to cover the prisons.

Now it is a disgrace that some parents have taken their discipline rights to an all-time low in today's society and are using our children as *punching bags*. My solution to that would be to take that parent into a room with some 6'5", 300 pound individuals and administer the same beating given to that child!

Discipline should be administered in a manner such as: "you have been disobedient in the area of …, and because I love you…." not, "I'm sick of your mess I'm going to tear you up." In the latter example, you have not taken the time to explain the reasoning for your discipline. Now some of you might say, "I don't have to explain," but that's an ungodly attitude to take for the Word of God says that you are to *"train up a child…"*

Parents often only focus on the discipline factor of this scripture (sure, I say beat 'em), but let's look at what else train means.

Webster's definition of train is: to direct the growth of, by bending, pruning, and tying (as in a plant); to form by instruction, discipline, or drill; to teach so as to make fit, qualified, or proficient; to make prepared for a test or skill.

Vine's Expository says this about <u>train</u> - it is translated as sober-minded - the Greek translation is "sophron" (sozo = to save, phren = the mind) - sophronizo denotes "to recall to one's senses," the training would involve the cultivation of sound judgment and prudence.

So you see, training means more than just showing your child where the *rod* is kept on the back of the bedroom door. It means also teaching them manners and etiquette, how to carry oneself in a professional manner, how to carry oneself as a gentleman or a lady, and how a young lady should sit and carry herself in public. Young boys need to be taught how to open a car door for a young lady, how to pull out her chair when sitting down at a table. Chivalry does not have to be dead!

We need to learn to slow down, take time and live. We live in a society that revolves around fully loaded microwaves, an environment of instantaneousness! We have instant potatoes, rice, cookies, oatmeal, dinner, lunch, this and that, even instant sex (I'm not sure where that came from, but some husband or wife just shouted hallelujah - smile).

Because of this fast paced society we live in, each generation's eating habits have greatly deteriorated. From fast foods to frozen foods, the upcoming generations have not been taught to cook anything from *scratch* because our busy schedules won't allow us. Therefore, it results in a generation of children that are vastly overweight and under nourished. My pastor always says, that, "we are raising a generation of *quarter pounders* and *biggy fries.*"

Mothers no longer teach their daughters the *art of homemaking*. Homemaking skills are a lost art in our society. We can thank the *ERA* (Equal Rights Amendments) through the feminist movement for that. It is now sexist to teach your daughter how to sew, clean and cook. You had better teach them, for there is nothing worse than a lazy woman. She might not leave home and then you would be stuck with a 37 year old *"slouch."* (I don't think that God made a mistake when Titus 2: 3-5 was dropped in the bible.)

I must admit that even though I was a latch-key-kid, I knew how to prepare a meal from beginning to end. A lot of my cooking skills came from watching my aunts and just experimenting. Mostly experimenting, particularly if I wanted to eat a meal before my mother came home from work. I learned the art of surviving.

Some from the baby boomer generation (1950's) and most of the current generation worships the *microwave,* and indulges often at *Ruby Tuesday's, Houlihan's, Mick's, McDonald's, Taco Bell, Burger King, and Chick-fil-A*, or whatever restaurant serves something fast.

Now I know that I've made a lot of you twenty-first century women mad, but that's O.K. Married women try cooking a meal and cleaning your house and see if your husband's head won't spin. By the way, if you didn't know, I'll tell you, a large percentage of divorces are a result of finances, with infidelity always ranking #1. Take care of your man's needs, the other woman knows how!

Single women bake a cake for the next covered dish event at the single's ministry and see if some heads don't go up.

Young and older single ladies if you expect to get married, *NEWS FLASH* - if you want that man to bring something to the table, you had better make sure that you have something to lay on it as well. Because surely when he's hungry, your fine looks won't feed him. You had better make sure that you can boil water - at least you can throw an egg or spaghetti in it.

Training entails a lot more than just using the rod. It calls for men and women of wisdom to raise children in today's society. The Bible offers some timeless advise of wisdom passed down by one father of old.

Fatherly Advice

On the subject of teen pregnancy, a Washington, DC author states, "the United States has the highest rate of teen pregnancy and births in the western industrialized world. Teen pregnancy costs the United States at least $7 billion annually." (The National Campaign to Prevent Teen Pregancy, 1997. *Whatever Happened to Childhood?* The Problem of Teen Pregnancy in the United States, Washington, DC Author).

Statistic generated from the Alan Guttmacher Institute states, "nearly four in 10 young women become pregnant at least once before they reach the age of 20 – nearly one million a year - (Analysis of Henshaw, S.K., *U.S. Teenage Pregnancy Statistics*, New York: Alan Guttmacher Institute, May, 1996; and Forest, J.D., *Proportion of U.S. Women Ever Pregnant Before Age 20,* New York: Alan Guttmacher Institute, 1986, unpublished).

Further statistics site that 79% of pregnancies are to unmarried teens - (Martin, J.A., Hamilton, B.E., Ventura, S.J., Menacher, F. & Park, M.M. (2002). *Births: Final data for 2000.* National Vital Statistics Reports 50(5)).

It makes you wonder how many of these youth's fathers sat them down and gave them some fatherly advice. However, there was one wise father who offered Godly wisdom and advice to his children, that if heeded by today's children will spare them the experience of prison, drugs, prostitution, homosexuality and a life of crime. Let's look at what he said about wisdom.

The Greek word for wisdom is **Sophia** - the insight into the true nature of things; spiritual things, debased form or the natural sphere. **Phronésis** – "understanding, prudence," is the ability to discern modes of action with a view to their results. (*Vine's Complete Expository Dictionary of the Old and New Testament words*; W. E. Vine, Merrill F. Unger, William White, Jr.; Thomas Nelson Publishers, Pg. 678).

The Hebrew word for wisdom is **Hokmâ** – has the special meaning of "dexterity, skill" in an art. It also, and more generally, means intelligent, sensible, judicious, endued with reason and using it; skillful to judge; skill in civil matters. (*The New Unger's Bible Dictionary*; Merrill F. Unger; Moody Press, Page 1369).

> **Sâkal** – to "be prudent, circumspect."
>
> **Tûshîyâ** – (properly "uprightness"), counsel; understanding.
>
> **Bînâ** – ("understanding"), the faculty of insight, intelligence.

Wisdom brings honor:

When a child is taught and adheres to the godly instructions of a father or a mother, as the years advance, the benefits are respect in your community and favor in many circles of influence.

> *Proverbs 1:8-9 - My son, hear the instruction of thy father, and forsake not the law of thy mother. For they shall be an ornament of grace unto thy head, and chains about thy neck.*

Wisdom preserves from disaster:

The proper counsel and instructions from parents regarding selection of friends results in choosing godly lifestyles, or friends, not relationships of destruction that lead to prison, drugs, prostitution, gangs, etc.

> *Proverbs 1:10, 15-16 - My son, if sinners entice thee, consent thou not. My son, walk not thou in the way with them; refrain thy foot from their path; For their feet run to evil, and make haste to shed blood.*

Wisdom delivers from evil:

Corporate fraud is a "buzz word" in the 21st century and it has become a common occurrence, all at the expense of obtaining riches. Parents must teach children that running after pipe dreams, gold, silver, big cars and other material stuff is not the sum of one's life. It is the hidden treasures of life – character, integrity, morals, and ethics, all of which are lacking in society.

> *Proverbs 2:1-2 - My son, if thou will receive my words, and hide my commandments with thee, So that thou incline thine ear unto wisdom, and apply thine heart to understanding;*

> *Proverbs 2:4,12 - If thou seekest her as silver, and searchest for her as for hidden treasures; To deliver thee from the way of the evil man, from men that speak [perverse] things.*

The rewards of wisdom:

When a child is taught wisdom, right thinking, proper judgment, and discernment of matters it keeps them alive. Teen drinking and driving has crept to the top of the death charts in the last year, cutting off lives that have so much purpose.

> *Proverbs 3:1-4 - My son, forget not my law, but let thine heart keep my commandments; For length of days, and long life, and peace, shall they add to thee. Let not mercy and truth forsake thee; bind them about thy neck; write them upon the table of thine heart; So shalt thou find favor and good understanding in the sight of God and man.*

Wisdom preserves from trouble:

> *Proverbs 4:10, 11, 14-15 - Hear my son, and receive my sayings, and the years of thy life shall be many. I have taught thee in the way of wisdom; I have led thee in right paths. Enter not into the path of the wicked, and go not in the way of evil men. Avoid it, pass not by it, turn from it, and pass away.*

Wisdom produces health:

One of many words of wisdom I could have used during my season as a homosexual were the physical consequences associated with the sexual practices that I partook in. But I believe this scripture even reflects spiritual health as well. There is nothing greater than having a healthy relationship, but it has to be taught.

> *Proverbs 4:20-22 - My son, attend to my words; incline thine ear unto my sayings. Let them not depart from thine eyes; keep them in the midst of thine heart. For they are life unto those that find them, and health to all their flesh.*

Wisdom will keep you from immorality:

This scripture offers such a loud warning to the young as well as the old. The strange woman could be a prostitute, a carnal wife, or anyone or anything that lures you into immorality with its smooth words, and clever sounding sales pitch. Tell your children, warn them, and beseech them to turn the other way. That road will destroy them.

> *Proverbs 5:1-7 - My son, attend unto my wisdom, and bow thine ear to my understanding, that thou mayest regard discretion, and that thy lips may keep knowledge. For the lips of a strange woman drop as an honeycomb, and her mouth is smoother than oil, But her end is bitter as wormwood, sharp as a two-edged sword. Her feet go down to death; her steps take hold on hell. Lest thou shouldest ponder the path of life, her ways are [unstable], that thou canst not know them. Hear me now therefore, O ye children, and depart not from the words of my mouth.*

Wisdom will preserve you from foolish financial entanglement:

So many people have lost money in bad financial investments, mainly due to the fact of poor or no financial education. During the last twenty years, co-signing has been a common financial agreement that people are binding to;

pushing many to great financial ruin, not to mention broken relationships. Parents must teach children how to be wise in their financial dealings.

> _Proverbs 6:1-4_ - _My son, if thou be surety for thy [neighbor], if thou hast [struck] thy hand with a stranger, thou are snared with the words of thy mouth, thou art taken with the words of thy mouth. Do this now, my son, and deliver thyself, when thou art come into the hand of thy [neighbor]: go, humble thyself, and [importune thy neighbor]._

Wisdom will keep you from being seduced:

> _Proverbs 7:1,5_ - _My son, keep my words, and lay up my commandments with thee. That they may keep thee from the strange woman, from the [foreigner] who flattereth with her words._

> _Please note: It is suggested that you read the New International Version (NIV) of the above scripture reference - it brings greater clarity._

CHOICES

CHOICES

> The farmer will make a predetermined decision ahead of time on what type of crops will be harvested. When he plants corn, he expects for corn to grow, not squash. When the farmer sells the corn crop to the supermarket, it's corn. No matter if the grocer advertises squash, if it looks like and taste like corn, it's corn.

We often make choices that do not line up with God's purpose and plan. And no matter how we dress it up or explain it away, if it is not God's original intent based on His word, it's sin. That's lifestyle, career, marriage, etc.

If she won't, someone else will!

My mother was very demanding and placed high expectations on me, which I found very difficult to live up to as a teenager. (In more recent years I have learned not to succumb to the pressure.) These high expectations brought further strife and turmoil between us. I felt that I could not do anything right in her eyes that would make her love me, draw closer to me, or give me that mother's love that I was so desperately seeking and wanting. My mother was cold and aloof. I often wished that she would have just *aborted* me. She was a nurse. She had the connections to get it done. Oh, but I'm glad she didn't. This book would never have been written.

In my search for love I found someone who was willing to give me *the perverted* version of that love. I often would try and explain my plight to my cousins. Their response to me was always, "she's your mother." I knew they couldn't understand for their mother was there for them. They have never known the pain and agony of an abusive mother. When the school bell rang at three o'clock p.m., their mother was home awaiting their arrival when they returned from school.

I began to search for love in all the wrong places, until one day I found the *"wrong love* in the *wrong place."* One must realize that only God can meet our deepest need for love. Not a husband, significant other, aunt, uncle, teacher, friend or a lover.

I choose!

Homosexuals come in all packages. The ones that are bold in their choice are more identifiable. They come from all walks of life (singers, preachers, doctors, lawyers, deacons, evangelists) you get the point. They are not always the person you think that is gay; somewhat like a pedophile, you may never suspect them. Even some who will read this book and hold prominent positions in the church are still in the lifestyle. A word of warning, GET OUT! We already know people of the world think it's O.K., but God says, "it's sin."

Six years ago, one lady made a comment to a women's group, she said "I just can't figure that one out," she was referring to lesbians. And you know, the sad part is that she will never understand something unless she's been in it.

My eight-year tap dance of death and destruction began at about age 16. I guest you can say the plunge into destruction. For prior to age sixteen, I flirted with some of the acts, and messed around with a couple of girls. Now I know some of your tongues have dropped to the floor by now, pick them up. Eight years is a long time to be in anything, drugs, prostitution, prison, etc.

The sexual emotion alone is a strong one that you just can't turn on and off at will. Well, the pull of homosexuality is just as strong, so intense, its a prison with bars that are locked shut. To be in such a debilitating state - only the power of God can deliver you.

I was not born this way. It was not a "chemical imbalance," nor was it an "over abundance of genes." That's a lie straight from the very pit of hell. I chose this! Circumstances and environment may have pushed me to the door, but I chose to go in.

Genesis 1:27 says *"So God created man in his own image, in the image of God created he him; male and female created he them."*

In all honesty I did not set out to be a *Lesbian* (a female homosexual, other street names, include butch, dike (or dyke) or bulldaggers). That was not my intent. I was not proud of it. As a matter of fact, I didn't want to tell anybody. It even took a while to admit to myself that I was a lesbian. I actually thought that because I was a Christian, it was not so bad. I fell for the deceptive lie that "God gave me these feelings, it must be o.k." I even went as far to make a ridiculous vow with my *lover* (the individual that a lesbian or gay person is involved with). We vowed that we would take our secret to the grave. I forgot to read <u>Proverbs 28:13</u> *"He that covereth his sins shall not prosper, but whoso confesseth and forsaketh them shall have mercy."*

I wanted to be loved. I wanted attention and affirmation. At this point, I was willing to get it anyway, or anyhow, and by any means necessary. Emotionally I was bankrupt, empty. This person (I'll call her Jean) gave me the attention that I was not able to get from anyone else. She listened to me. She would hold me when I needed to be held. That was the crux of our relationship. The sexual part was minute, but it was very much there and that made the relationship sinful. It was a choice that I made.

I knew that my lifestyle was wrong. I was ashamed but I just could not get out of it. Being young and vulnerable did not help. I was very impressionable, very easily persuaded. This is why teen homosexuality is escalating. They want love and attention. They are vulnerable. Most teens will have lovers who are older than they are. The teen is looking for a mother/father type person. Someone older represents that parent they tried to get love from.

Just look at the current revelation and exposure of sexual misconduct and pedophile activities by Catholic priests that has been revealed in the news. All the violations were upon children and teens at their most vulnerable state. So trusting of an adult and their authority that they have to succumb their innocence to the most heinous act upon a child.

Is He, or is She?

There are many obvious traits that characterize homosexuals and then there have been the stereotypical traits, some of which still remain amongst some of the homosexual population.

Formerly, the woman wore the *butch* haircuts (shaved down, little on top nothing on sides and back). Now ladies, I'm not saying that short hair is representative of being a lesbian. Some women just have problems growing hair. However, formerly on the *circuit*, the butch cut was and for some still is, the identifier. Also, wearing large baggy, manly clothing; taking on the characteristic of male behavior including rough talking and sitting with your legs spread, mannish conversation, and trying to be one of the boys. Put you in a group of men and you blend right in. Still in some instances you will see the more brazen lesbians grabbing their genitals like some men do (which by the way, is very rude, even when a man does it).

Today, there is the highly professional, white-collar lesbian. She dresses for success, may have long fingernails and wear high heels, but she still tries to act like a man when the heels come off.

Male homosexuals are called *"Gay,"* (known on the street as, faggots, queers, queens, or fairies). In prior years and even some today wear their hair tinted (get it dyed back), it's an "attention getter." Colored contacts are used to enhance the eyes, to make you more attractive to another man. Also the soft voices (speak-up men), long fingernails, certain style suits and loud colors are all used to draw attention. Men I'm not saying a bright suit is wrong but again it is an identifier. It makes you stand out in the crowd, particularly if you are on the *hunt* (for another gay).

Today, as with the lesbian, there is the high profile professional and the white-collar gay male. You even have the burley football player who is now "coming out." And the very strong athletic type is not exempt either. There are platoon partners laying in ditches with other platoon members, who will get out of the ditch and return to their barracks, only to hop in the bed with their lovers (don't ask, don't tell). Then there is the new wave of individuals called "MSM" (Men Who Have Sex With Men). This particular group does not identify themselves as homosexuals; they just like having sex with men.

Then there are some traits that are just not as obvious, only to a person who has been in homosexuality. Some homosexuals are not practicing the lifestyle, however, they are carrying around a homosexual *spirit* (mannerisms, mindset and the such). There is a certain spirit that exudes, a spirit that other homosexuals know. And if you are carrying that spirit you just can't go to certain places or be in certain environments. The entire *spirit of homosexuality* has to be brought under the blood of Jesus Christ, annihilated if you will. If I can use an analogy: when a dog urinates he likes to go back to that same spot or somewhere near it, he sniffs it out. Homosexuals can sniff out other homosexuals, they know where they are. They know whose church has the largest population; they know where the homosexuals frequent.

And in case you did not know - *!NEWS FLASH!* - Homosexuality permeates the House of God like you wouldn't believe. The music industry both secular and religious is full of homosexuals. In the church, the choir can be a *breeding* ground. It's a place to get attention, a place where you feel accepted, a place you can hide. In quite a few churches, choir members are free to come and go at will; there is very little accountability past the colored curtain railing of the choir loft.

Females make up 70-80% of the population in choirs. This makes an appetizing smorgasbord for the lesbian to choose from. What better place to find a woman? Other than an all-male choir, the male population is often small in the choir, therefore, making it quite easy to point out the gay prospect. The church as a whole is a great pick-up place. Individuals are church going, focused on spirituality, trusting, and perhaps dedicated and committed. These are attributes wanted in any partner. Homosexuals are not likely to find an abusive partner in the church, so the church becomes a *"safe house"* for homosexual partner selection.

Quite some years ago, there was a certain male group (and I say this with reservation) of singers who could sing, but they were all gay and very comfortable in their lifestyle, and with what appeared to be no convictions. They use their appearance to attract men, bright colors, tinted hair, colored contacts, and earrings – these were all "signs".

Paul says in I Thessalonians 4:22 *"Abstain from all appearance of evil."*

During my childhood, any man wearing an earring in his ear was a sign (a mockery was made of him). Whispers filled the street as he walked passed for everyone knew that he was *gay*, sissy as we called them. Now everybody wears one. Men "come up in the church" wearing them, they even have crosses dangling from the ear making it look, I guess spiritual. *You had better check what it represents before you wear it*! Being an ex-homosexual makes me qualified to say this, I've been there, to hell and back, a few hundred times! I know the look.

There is a concentrated population of homosexuals (both gays and lesbians) in the music departments of churches and secular industries. However, that is not to say homosexuals don't populate other areas of industries (particularly the arts as a whole); television, and church ministries.

Usher Board, don't you get too snobbish. You have them too! Prayer Ministry, you're not exempt. They lurk amongst you as well. They pray with emotion and fervency. Eloquent speech just rolls right off their lips. Oh, they know how to say it. Homosexuals are everywhere, in every line of business, profession, and ministry. And yes, they are even in the pulpit! There are churches established just for homosexuals and their partners.

The spirit of homosexuality permeates the church with such impact! I'm reminded of how terrible a job some (not all) parents have done, Christians included, in raising their offspring. Also, the Church has done a terrible job in speaking out against homosexuality- just keeping silent, even in the pulpit. And worst yet, many churches sanction this immoral behavior. Metropolitan Community Church was founded by Troy Perry in 1968, largely for practicing homosexuals. The United Church of Christ (UCC), some of the Episcopalian Churches, and Unitarian-Universalist Association Churches, just to name a few have openly practicing homosexual clergy. For your convenience, there is also a magazine for gay and lesbian Christians and it has a multi-page listing of Christian churches and organizations.

If you have young children in your home, now is the time to evaluate what you are speaking into you child. If they are teens, and you have messed up in nurturing them, there is still hope; it takes an even greater effort and hard work on your part. But I am reminded that *"God is able to do exceedingly and abundantly........"* Ephesians 3:20.

As I sit in church services and watch ushers, choir members, band members, and members alike, and as the worship leaders get up *batting their eyes* and *bending their wrists*, it sends a knife piercing my heart. When I peruse the Christian television stations, there are men of God standing proclaiming God's word and their fingernails and hair dos look better than mine. I observe women of God, with such rough exteriors, nothing feminine about them. I'm reminded of one, well acclaimed, powerful, dynamic speaker, but the spirit of homosexuality hovers around her - like a dog around a fire hydrant.

When will the church start to look differently than the world?

In the church, youth and adults (both male and female) are being "turned out" by same sex partners the night before, then go and lead worship; usher our seniors and youths to their seats; pray for our needs; and even stand and proclaim God's righteousness in the pulpit. The church is a meeting place, a pick up joint; a "praying church" has now become the "flaming sanctuary." Men are on the hunt! Women are on the hunt! If Matthew 21:13 were re-written it would read: *"My house shall be called the house of prayer, but you have made it a den of flaming folk."*

When will the church put out the fires that burn with sexual perversion inside its four walls?

Who are they on the inside?

Some homosexuals are often characterized as having a *Melancholy Temperament*. Some are characterized with a *Choleric Temperament*, and God forbid if you are in a relationship with one. They are possessive and controlling to the end. They will make you feel guilty if you try to get out of the relationship. Some male homosexuals are characterized by indecisiveness, and inability to make decisions at crucial times.

I possess a Chlor-Mel (Choleric and Melancholy) temperament (more information is given regarding recommended reading on temperaments in Chapter 9). The Choleric personalities can be very domineering, controlling and manipulative. While the Melancholy personality is pessimistic, moody, and self-centered. I was very possessive and wanted to consume all of "Jean's" time. When she couldn't meet that demand and give me the time I needed, I would often accuse her of using me. Probably in some instances she was. However, I was obsessed with "Jean."

I would resort to using finances as a manipulative way to obtain her affection and attention, and at times it worked. However, sometimes this backfired and I would be even more frustrated than when I started out.

This obsessive spending led to a lot of my debt problems. I did not always intentionally use money and gifts to be manipulative in the relationship. Sometimes, I honestly thought that "Jean" would love me more and that I needed to do more if I wanted more out of her. Those are the times the melancholy took over.

Jean possessed some of the Choleric temperament in that she often controlled things and she knew how to push certain buttons when she wanted certain material things out of me or wanted me to do certain things for her (errands, work, etc.).

Oftentimes in a Chlor-Mel personality, even though we possess one of the characteristics of manipulation, it is mislabeled or misunderstood (our actions, works or motives). The things that we do that are considered manipulation, often is the Melancholy trait ruling. We sometimes do things for approval, not to take advantage. You will really have to know a person before you can make that snap judgment.

One of the weak character traits of a Melancholy personality is pessimism. This trait will cause the melancholy homosexual to die in their state because they will begin to believe that there is just no way out of that thing.

Melancholy people are also often creative and naturally gifted. That's how they end up in the *music department* or any other *creative ministry*.

I did not wear the butch haircut, wear baggy clothes or necessarily walk like a man, but for sure I was playing the part of the man. And at times I would become physically rough. If you saw me you probably would not have suspected it. I was a *closet homosexual*, living a double life. I would pray daily that no one would find out. I lived in constant fear of someone finding out and in the desperation of trying to get out.

I manifested a *"Jezebel"* spirit. (*Jezebel*, the wife of Ahab, was not only a treacherous woman, she slayed prophets, taunted poor Elijah, and died a horrible death. But Jezebel also represents a spirit. An evil spirit that hates men and the authority that God has ordained for them.) This spirit strategically plots and schemes to undermine the authority of a man and ultimately God's authority.

There is an order. <u>I Corinthians 11:2-3</u> - *"Now I praise you, brethren, that ye remember me in all things, and keep the ordinances, as I delivered them to you. But I would have you know that the head of every man is Christ; and the head of every woman is the man; and the head of Christ is God."*

We can debate this point until Christ returns, but God's word says it, and that just about settles it. Because we have gotten out of the order originated, we have complete chaos upon the earth. When women refuse to be what God has ordained for us to be, *nurturer* and *helpmeet*, we produce *second-class men*, both in the male gender and in the female gender.

I have come to learn that I don't have to climb a telephone pole, pull a fire hose, run an obstacle course in boot camp, or drill a hole in the streets to prove my power and capabilities. Some feminist movements are derived out of a woman's insecurities in who she is. Don't you know that God has given women *"great power"* and when used correctly we can obtain anything? Don't forget the old saying, *"The hand that rocks the cradle, rules the world."* That has not changed, but instead, women want to rock other things.

You know, it was a group of *Jezebel female activists* who wanted to protest the *Promise Keepers March*. <u>Promise Keepers</u> is a group of men who dare to be men and take the seat of authority that God has given them. In October 1997, these men of God rallied together in our nation's capitol, Washington, D.C., to reclaim their God-given positions. A few feminists got together and formed their little group in protest. Ladies, such a silly display of insecurity. If a man wants to stand up and be the man he is supposed to be, let him. That takes a lot of stress off of women. Check your medical condition for the last twenty or so years; stress, balding, heart disease, hypertension, cancer. You name it, we've got it. Undue stress brings on many of these conditions. You won't lose anything by letting a man exercise godly authority. But you'll gain all!

Now I did not actually hate men, but I had a strong competitive spirit towards them. I lacked respect for their position. I could do just as well as a man or better, I thought. So I guess I did hate them. I did not know what to love about them. I never had a male figure in my life - only domineering, aggressive, and authoritative women.

I would challenge a man in a minute. I had no problems hitting a man if the situation warranted it. I might have ended up with a bloody nose or black eye, but I was not going out without a good fight, and I was sure to get at least one hit, kick or cut in.

Years ago I was seeing this guy who made a bet with me that he would get my "stuff" (I'm being as real as I can, O.K., have sex with me). We got into this heated argument and I went to turn and walk away from him. He grabbed me by my arm and before I knew it my hand met his face suddenly, if you get my point. That was the last I saw of him. At this point in my life, I had no problem being a second-class man, and I was sure to let you know who was wearing the pants in the relationship.

I had made the choice to live this immoral lifestyle! I had been given up to my own vile affections. Romans 1:26 says *"For this cause God gave them up unto vile affections; for even their women did exchange the natural use for that which is against nature."* I had given into my own lust and fleshly desires. James 1:14 says *"But every man is tempted, when he is drawn away of his own lust, and enticed."*

I made the choice, a poor decision at that, which drew me further away from God into things that just weren't natural, (sexual practices that were vile). Against the very nature and character of God. I saw, I desired and I was quickly drawn into.

IT'S JUST NOT NATURAL

IT'S JUST NOT NATURAL

> ### Hybrid
> In agriculture or horticultural, when you cross-breed sometimes you get something that does not look natural, something out of the ordinary. It's not what the farmer planted, or what was originally intended to be the outcome.

Men have told boys, "*real men don't cry*"; women have told girls "*all men are dogs.*" It's no wonder that each one will seek affection and affirmation from their own gender.

My mother's famous expression was, all men are dogs. Grant you that assumption came from the bad relationships that she had been involved in. However, she would then transfer that same negative spirit onto me. My mother obviously had sexual relationships with at least two men for my brother and I have different fathers. And because of her refusal to tell me about either of them, leads me to believe that she was hurt in some way by each. Also, the fact that she often commented to me that they were dogs. I do feel for her that she never was able to get to know a real man, what a loss.

Some Black men (I'm talking to the Black sisters) won't rise to the occasion because we beat them so low with our destructive tongues. Sometimes the brother gets beat down on the job, then the world system, at the church, and then comes home to it. This will have to change if we expect men of color, for that matter, any man to rise and be what God has ordained them to be.

On the flipside of things men, stop treating women like you don't need us or we don't know anything. Stop treating us as sex objects for sexual gain and/or prostituting us for your financial, social status or self gain, (in the church or outside the church).

I came up in the era where women were fighting for equality (ERA), but that's what my fellow sisters were forcing on me. Don't get me wrong, I believe in equal work, equal pay. However, a woman carrying a rifle on her shoulder just does not look natural. God called men to protect, not women. "Please open my door and pull my chair out." I don't care what the second-class man says. I like it! It's an age-old issue that started in the Garden of Eden. (See Genesis 3: 1-6) The woman still wants control and authority.

Although today sexual harassment can take place anywhere and amongst any gender, it still more frequently takes place in male environments - firefighters, army, coal mines, truckers, police force, etc.

Don't go over there!

There was a three-year-old boy who played in his yard every day. The yard was closed in by a 6ft. solid wood fence. The child's mother told him that he was not to go outside of the fence. Each day the little boy would get a glimpse of the fast moving cars and trucks swishing past his fence. What the child did not understand is that the fence was not necessarily to keep him in, but to keep danger out. Furthermore, on the other side of the fence was a huge hill that led directly to the highway of fast moving cars and trucks, but the child did not know that. The little boy opened the fence gate and he plummeted into danger instantly.

Society today is very much like that little boy. We are doing things that are morally out of bounds. I, too, was like that little boy; I opened the fence gate and walked into an ungodly lifestyle that caused me to plummet into a demoralizing state of being. The homosexual lifestyle was a result of the sexual exposure and abuse that I had glimpsed of through my fence.

With the introduction of the "*Big Kiss*" on *Roseanne* in the mid-nineties; January 1997, the ABC drama *Relativity* which included a lesbian scene with caressing, nuzzling and passionate, open-mouthed kissing, and the coming out of Ellen DeGeneres in May 1997, sitcoms are glorifying homosexuality and down-playing the great consequences of this sick and twisted lifestyle.

And by no means is there a shortage of gay/lesbian literature (how to, when to, where to). Scores and scores of books, journals, periodicals, and magazines have lined the bookshelves in Bookstores and Libraries, all in support of this sinful lifestyle.

Let me pause to settle some things right here, right now. I am not suffering from homophobia (defined as a fear, dislike, or hatred of homosexuals). I am not a gay-basher. I do not want to see any living human or animal abused because of what they believe. I do not support Gay Rights, and certainly not at the expense of children being influenced by the lifestyle, such as with the gay rights agenda in some public schools. The New York City Public School's curriculum had included four pro-homosexual books aimed at the young. "*Heather Has Two Mommies*" is a book about a lesbian couple having a child through artificial insemination. "*Daddy's Roommate*" is a book about a boy with divorced parents who visits his father and his father's new male roommate. *"Gloria Goes to Gay Pride"* is a book that expresses choices, women loving women, men loving men.

The rationale of these books is found on page 145 of the city's *"Children of the Rainbow"* first-grade curriculum, which states that a teacher must "be aware of varied family structures, including gay or lesbian parents," and "children must be taught to acknowledge the positive aspects of each type of household." (John Leo, *"Heather Has a Message"*, U.S. News & World Report, 17 August 1992, p.16).

There is nothing positive about a gay household. As if a first grader doesn't already have enough problems trying to learn to tie his shoe, now they are being given these types of situations to adapt and adjust to.

Peter LaBarbera in an article for Family Research Council-Insight lists:

The Top 10 Strategies Used By Homosexual Activists in Schools.
(www.frc.org/insight).

1. **Promote victim status; exploit "safety" rhetoric**.
   …appeals for pro-homosexuality school programs is the idea that "gay youth" are victims in need of special protection by school administrators.

2. **Start with very young children**.
   …homosexual activists seek to change cultural norms by targeting society's youngest members with the ideology. …homosexual advocates have taken to promoting "tolerance" of "gays" and "lesbians"…

3. **Discuss alternative "families"/celebrate "diversity."**
   …beginning with very young students, encourage discussion of homosexual-led families as normal. Debra Chasnoff, a lesbian and co-producer of the video *It's Elementary: Talking about Gay Issues in School* – which shows grade-school children receiving pro-homosexuality lessons in class…

4. **Enact school nondiscrimination codes.**
   …add "sexual orientation" to the nondiscrimination codes

of school districts, school boards, education-oriented professional associations and other institutions to lay the groundwork for further pro-homosexuality efforts.

5. **Promote "coming out" and GLBT (Gay, Lesbian, Bisexual and Transgender) Pride.**
Grooming young students for "coming out" as homosexuals, bisexuals and transgenders is a central plank of the homosexual education movement.

6. **Encourage (and fund) pro-homosexuality student clubs**.
...formaton of school-based "Gay-Straight Alliances" (GSAs), which are de facto homosexuality booster and prograganda clubs.

Every year, the Commission on gay and lesbian youth helps bus "gay, lesbian, bisexual and transgender" students from across the state to Boston for a pro-homosexuality pep rally on the steps of the state capitol (Jim Hanes, ***Youth Pride Days Hails New 'Gay' School Groups***," CultureFacts, May 22, 1999, reporting on the Fifth Annual "Gay/Straight Youth Pride Rally" at the state capitol in Boston, May 7, 1999).

7. **Adopt Homosexuality-Affirming Curricula.**
In high schools and colleges, the main tactics have been to stress that famous historical figures were "gay", even if there is no definitive proof for the claim.

8. **Use openly homosexual teachers and "role models."**
Homosexual activist now assert their "right" to be open about their homosexuality to the students in their care.

9. **Pro-homosexuality counseling for troubled youth.**
...many young men and women are encouraged to embrace a "gay" sexual identity by their school counselors.

The American School Counselor Association now endorses the claim of a natural and "unalterable" homosexual identity for "sexual minority" youth (See the American School Counselor Association's position statement on "*The Professional School Counselor and Sexual Minority Youth*" at the organization's website, www.schoolcounselor.org).

10.   **Equate opposition with hate, bigotry and prejudice.**

I am not in support of same sex marriages. God's Word says in Genesis 2:22-24 - "*And the rib, which the Lord God had taken from man, made he a woman, and brought her unto the man. And Adam said, This is now bone of my bones, and flesh of my flesh; she shall be called Woman, because she was taken out of Man. Therefore shall a man leave his father and his mother, and shall cleave unto his wife; and they shall be one flesh.*" God brought the **woman** unto the **man**; **not** the **man unto** the **man**, **nor** the **woman unto** the **woman**. Same sex marriages are in total violation of God's Word. Regardless of how special that person makes you feel.

Yes, I do have a burden for the homosexual because I know how the lifestyle destroyed me. I know someone has just responded, "well that's you," no, that's you as well. Proverbs 16:25 says "*There is a way that seemeth right unto a man, but the end thereof are the ways of death.*" If the lifestyle has not already begun to destroy you emotionally, physically, financially and spiritually, it will.

There is a new phrase that has been coined, "*Alternative Lifestyle.*" There is no alternative in the sight of God. You're either **male** or **female**. My Pastor, Bishop Eddie L. Long says, "check the plumbing, do I have a vagina, or do I have a penis?" You see, your parts won't lie. But your mind will. Remember, we are taught that seeing is believing. So tell me, what do you see?

Homosexuality is taught in our public school systems under the disguise of "*multi-culturalism.*" Perhaps you think that's why God wanted parents to teach their own children (Deuteronomy 6:6-9)? You think that perhaps God knew that society would become depraved?

In junior and high school, there was a classmate named Karen. She was an "A & B" student, a very pleasant girl to know. But by high school, Karen became a troublemaker in class. She frequently got into street brawls; she began smoking cigarettes as well as reefer (marijuana). By the time we graduated she had converted to a full-fledge lesbian. She had the butch haircut, she wore baggy clothes; she stopped wearing a bra (she had large breast which made them more noticeable). Even her voice began to change; she started talking low. If your back were turned to her, you would have sworn it was a man talking. I often wondered what things were associated with her environment that prompted the conversion. Seeing Karen and knowing her prior to her conversion, it just didn't seem natural.

Look at what you're doing!

Let me first point out that even though homosexuality is a sin, there is forgiveness and deliverance for all who turn to Jesus Christ. Secondly, I want to point out that homosexuality is *abnormal behavior*. It is abnormal because God did not create the woman for the woman or the man for the man.

On August 30, 1991, Peri Jude Radecic, a member of the National Gay and Lesbian Task Force stated on the ABC news show *Nightline*: "Homosexuality is not an illness, it is not something that needs to be cured. We are normal, natural and healthy people."

Romans 1:26 says, *"For this cause God gave them up unto vile affections; for even their woman did [exchange] the natural use for that which is against nature."*

Well Peri, I beg the differ. There was nothing normal, natural or healthy about me as a lesbian *sucking, fondling or caressing another woman's breast; fondling, rubbing or licking her vagina, or French kissing, all used to arouse sexual excitement and eventually lead to an orgasm.* The only "female to female breast sucking" that should occur in a female's life is from birth to two years of age (or three years of age in some cases).

There is nothing normal or natural about two women snuggled together on a couch or in a bed, two women taking a shower or bath together, two women entwined in the nude feeling, caressing and fondling one another. There is nothing natural or healthy about a woman placing her fingers into another woman's vagina, to be representative of a penis and used to produce an orgasm. (The vagina has been designed for the penis and the delivery of a baby. I'm still questioning the "*speculum*," the instrument used in a pelvic examine. Why is such a violent instrument used? But that's research for another book.)

Speaking of the holding and caressing, I am not referring to a mother holding a daughter, or an aunt holding a niece or any female another female with the intent to comfort or console. I'm referring to this type of behavior with sexual intent. For God designed females to be nurturers.

There is nothing normal, natural or healthy about a gay male having anal or oral intercourse. Anal intercourse (sodomy) involves foreign objects inserted into the rectum for an erotic sensation. Oral intercourse (fellatio), the tongue is used to lick or tickle the outlet of the rectum for sexual excitement, arousing or foreplay. Also, the oral sex would involve the sucking or fondling of the penis to achieve an ejaculation and orgasm.

Then there are other activities known as *"Fisting"* and *"Water Sports."* Fisting involves a fisted hand being inserted into the rectum that would produce various sexually exciting sensations. Water Sports involves urinating into the mouth or rectum, to cause a sexual stimulation.

Because of the small size of the anus, some type of drug-induced state may need to occur to reduce the amount of pain. The anus was designed for the elimination of body waste, not vibrators, soda bottles, sticks or light bulbs.

In an article entitled "Medical Perspective of the Homosexual Issue", written by Dr. Bernard J. Klamecki, a proctologist (rectal specialist) and a well-known medical professional among the homosexual community, he stated, *"persistent anal-rectal sexual activity can lead to various pre-cancerous lesions such as Bowen's disease and Kaposi's sarcoma. Whenever tissues are traumatized, cracked, or abraded, they are vulnerable to bacterial infection."*

Now what makes these practices unhealthy are the following: they can affect the oral cavities (abscesses), lungs, penis, prostate, bladder, anus, perianal areas outside of the rectum (tissues can be cracked or traumatized), rectum, colon, vagina (infections), uterus, pelvic area (violent activities can tear muscles), brain, skin (lesions), blood, immune system, and other body systems. Let us not forget the various bacterial and viral diseases, the most prominent of which is AIDS (Acquired Immune Deficiency Syndrome).

In the same article as mentioned above, Dr. Klamecki stated, *"the current figure is that 70 percent of Americans with AIDS are male homosexuals or bisexuals."*

AIDS is not just a single disease but a syndrome of one or more diseases brought on by the Human Immunodeficiency Virus (HIV). Two common diseases are pneumocystis carinii and Kaposi's sarcoma.

AIDS is a disease that is transmitted by the exchange of blood and/or body fluids. If I have not said anything else to compel someone to come out of the lifestyle, perhaps the aforementioned diseases will. AIDS not only affects adults, but children are now being ravaged by this deadly epidemic. When entire nations are being destroyed through reckless sexual behavioral lifestyles, it is no longer just *your business*, how you live your life. The *condom* will not protect you.

Not only are homosexual practices unhealthy, but also the homosexual is three times more suicidal than the heterosexual, as recorded in a study of the life expectancy of homosexual men and women – Paul Cameron, William L. Playfair, and Stephen Wellum, *"The Homosexual Lifespan"*; Family Research Institute, 14 February 1992.

I firmly support this statement due to my many suicidal attempts during the period of my homosexual lifestyle. There is a lot of pressure that comes with this lifestyle, one being the many medical concerns of contracting a fatal disease, second, for me the fear of someone finding out. Today's homosexuals sometimes live with the fear of being physically abused because of their sexual preferences and/or orientation. These two alone can cause depression and more times than not, suicidal attempts, especially in teens.

God calls the sexual practices of the homosexual <u>unnatural</u>. <u>Romans 1:27-28</u> says *"And likewise also the men, leaving the natural use of the woman, burned in their lust one toward another, men with men working that which is unseemly, and receiving in themselves that recompense of their error which was [fitting]. And even as they did not like to retain God in their knowledge, God gave them over to a reprobate mind, to do those things which are not [seemly]."*

The Lord further called it an <u>abomination</u>. <u>Leviticus 18:22</u> says *"Thou shalt not lie with mankind, as with womankind: it is abomination."* <u>Abomination</u> means extreme disgust and hatred.

In the Old Testament homosexuality <u>warranted death</u>. <u>Leviticus 20:13</u> reads *"If a man also lie with mankind, as he lieth with a woman, both of them have committed an abomination: they shall surely be put to death; their blood shall be upon them."*

We must look at God's **original** purpose in creating human sexuality. It was for procreation, through the sexual union of a **married** man and woman for the reproduction of the human race; not through *test tubes* and *cloning* and other man-made methods. Genesis 1:27b-28 reads "...*Male and female he created them. And God blessed them, and God said unto them, Be fruitful, and multiply, and [fill] the earth, and subdue it....*"

It is only in the heterosexual union of marriage that we can fulfill God's intended order, not through homosexual relationships.

HARVEST TIME

HARVEST TIME

Harvesting

Harvest is a time that all farmers look forward to. The reaping of the crops take place. This will manifest the results of the farmer's labor. Depending on that year, a great harvest can be expected, or if conditions were bad, a not so great harvest can be expected.

Galatians 6:7-8 reads *"Be not deceived, God is not mocked, for whatever a man soweth, that shall he also reap. For he that soweth to his flesh shall of the flesh reap corruption; but he that soweth to the Spirit shall of the Spirit reap life everlasting."*

Let me assure you that homosexuality or any sin for that matter does not go by without consequences. It does not go without reaping a *bad harvest*. Some of the crops produced from my bad harvest are now being used to share with others the consequences of my lifestyle.

I was nineteen and working full-time with the Government and living in my own apartment. Slowly after beginning to get out of the lifestyle (around age 23) I became seriously ill. Initially it started with the contraction of *"Hepatitis A."* I was sick for months with the infection, for what seemed to be no end in sight.

Months later my body still had not been restored to full health. I began to rapidly lose weight. I went from 135 pounds to 110 within a matter of weeks. I couldn't keep foods down or in. It took what seemed to be months for the doctors to diagnose what I had. Leukemia (my white blood cell count was very low), AIDS, Rheumatoid Arthritis, and Multiple Sclerosis were among the diagnoses. My hearing was beginning to be affected. I suffered shortness of breath, mild seizures, and soon afterwards my eyesight began to worsen.

By this time I had been to see many doctors in the Pennsylvania area, a Neurosurgeon, Cancer Specialist, and Lung Specialist. I began to feel like the woman with the issue of blood. I had spent all my money! In April 1983, I had an appointment to see an eye specialist at one of the leading eye institutes in Pennsylvania. He recognized the disease. I was diagnosed with "*Sarcoidosis.*"

At the time of diagnoses, in 1983, there was very little research on this some-times-fatal disease. One of my primary doctors on the medical team from the University of Pennsylvania Hospital described the disease to me as follows: <u>Sarcoidosis</u> *is a disease found predominately amongst young black females. It is not communicable, and at the time there is no cure for it. It attacks tissues and organs and its final stage is death."* By then the dis-ease had claimed its territory in my body.

On April 26, 2002, the Henry Ford Health System (<u>www.henryford.com</u>) had on its website the following article on Sarcoidosis:

"Sarcoidosis Remains Mystery to Researchers"

Sarcoidosis (sar-koy-do-sis) is a disease that causes inflammation of the lungs and can also affect the eyes, skin, heart and other organs.

There is no known cause or cure.

"Sarcoidosis appears to be an abnormal immune response," said Michael Iannuzzi, M.D., senior staff pulmonologist at Henry Ford Hospital in Detroit, who is leading an $8 million National Institutes of Health (NIH) study on the disease.

Iannuzzi says, Sarcoidosis is much more prevalent in African Americans, especially women between the ages of 20 and 40.

A battery of testing was done to find out the extent of damage that the dis-ease had caused. CAT scans, gallium scans, a spinal tap, upper and lower GI, EKG, a pulmonary test, and all sorts of blood work presented their findings. The disease was focused and had damaged one lung, my liver, heart, and brain. I had problems with one of my legs; I would drag it. Soon thyroid problems developed.

It was during these few years that I had to quit my job and go on disability. I was unable to perform any duties due to mild seizures that were occurring, as well as other health problems. In August 1985, my doctor was planning to remove my thyroid; it was causing me so many problems. I would be on medication for the rest of my life.

During my sickness, I further slipped away from God. Mind you, He had not left me. Bible reading was sporadic; prayer was only out of necessity. I only wanted God to heal me. (My, isn't He faithful?) <u>I Corinthians 11:30</u> states *"For this cause many are weak and sickly among you, and many sleep (dead)."*

In my mess I still took communion, — don't play with God, He almost took me out of here!

My sickness brought months of anxiety. There were many weeks of hospital and doctor visits. The scores of tests that I had to endure were relentless, and I went through most of them alone. I even had one of the specialists tell me during one of my visits that "it was all in my mind." Needless to say, I was left with no string of hope to latch onto. I just wanted some answers to the pain and deterioration in my body. I felt at least if I had a diagnosis, then maybe I could handle all this a little better. When you are sick and going from doctor to doctor and not knowing what you have, it is torture to the mind. I thought that I was going to die and not know what I had died from. So when I was diagnosed, it was a relief.

You who may be reading this may be going through some illness, maybe from sin's consequences or perhaps for faith developing, don't give up. God has a plan for everything we will ever go through and when we submit our wills to His, then and only then can He work the healing process.

As I confessed my sins, submitted to God's will that is when the healing started taking place. Body part by body part. Soon my spirit would be healed, issue by issue.

<u>II Chronicles 7:14</u> says *"If my people, who are called by my name, shall humble themselves, and pray, and seek my face, and turn from their wicked ways, then will I hear from heaven, and will forgive their sin, and will heal their land."*

It seemed so dark!

The lifestyle of homosexuality was a dark time for me. Prior to my physical illness, I also experienced the mental illness of the lifestyle. It was during the reaping of my harvest, that I reached the end of my rope, caused by living with an abusive mother, sexual abuse, the homosexual lifestyle, the many location moves I faced as a child, the strained relationships and the loneliness. The lifestyle was just too much for me to take. I was distraught and I had just about all that I could take.

My life spiraled downward, then it crashed into the *pool of depression.* My bouts with depression were internalized. My nerves were frazzled. The doctor prescribed mild sedatives (Valium being one of them) for me to take to calm my nerves. My hands were always clammy. I would bite my nails down to the skin and I could not sleep at night. However, nerve pills just did not cut it and sleeping pills had the reverse effect for me.

Growing up as a child, I would characterize myself as very unhappy and withdrawn. I believe my bouts with depression started in the 7th grade and intensified by the end of my senior year of high school. I went through at least half of my life by then with little or no affirmation. I did not know who I was, what I was here for, or what matter it made that I was here. Just somebody, take away the pain.

I can remember sitting on the church steps in 1983 or so, crying, I was so distraught and wanting a cousin of mine just to hold me. I was slipping away and no one knew the whole story.

It was in the latter 70's, early 80's that the more severe bouts with depression began. It was during that time also that I was practicing the homosexual lifestyle. The lifestyle contributed a lot to my emotional problems. With "Jean," my *partner, lover,* or whatever you want to call her, I was in a constant battle of personalities and power struggles. As I look back I find that a lot of the depression was guilt, the guilt of being in a homosexual lifestyle.

I was seventeen when I left home and nineteen when I got my own apartment. Prior to getting an apartment, I lived with my Aunt Ruth and also with an elderly couple. I was on my own then, and it was those nights in that lonely apartment that I made three suicidal attempts on my life, (at different times of course). Now mind you I did not want to die, I just wanted the pain to stop; I wanted someone to hear me, someone to care for me. I wanted to be given a special place in someone's life. No strings attached, no hidden agendas, no hidden motives.

Things seemed so dark to me. My nights were often tearful and sleepless. I was being tormented by little creatures (now I know them to be *imps*). They would taunt me at night telling me that I could not live without "Jean." They would tell me that if I got out of the relationship Jean would tell everybody what I did. They would tell me, Jean was all I had. They would tell me, if you go to sleep, you will die. That is why most nights were sleepless, I did not want to die in my sleep; but yet I was trying to kill myself, go figure.

Depression is nothing to be taken lightly, parents, teachers, and leaders (especially in the church) need to know the warning signs of child and teenage depression. There are always signs; most adults just don't know them.

One cold winter night, the air was raw outside and the atmosphere inside was just as cold. I made my first suicide attempt by *slashing my wrist*. Afterwards, I panicked. I still bear the scar. It is somewhat faded now, but enough remains to remind me of God's undying love and grace in my life.

My second attempt was with *nail polish remover* — oh how it burned going down! It took months for the burning sensation to cease. Every time I swallowed something, it was very painful.

The last attempt (I'm not going to say the final, for I had experienced in some years after those attempts, some suicidal thoughts) was an *overdose of pills*. By then I was on so much medication for the Sarcoid, I could assist with my own death, who needed *"Dr. Kevorkian?"*

Sometimes I would walk around in a daze, life just passed me by quickly. I could not cope. It was during these suicidal times in my life that I was working for the Federal Government. A benefit as a government employee was the Employee Assistance Program (EAP), so I looked into the service. Mind you the very thought of going to a shrink was furthest from my mind and it was something that people in their right minds did not do. But at the time I wasn't in my right mind. I was a walking time bomb ready to detonate at any time.

I finally convinced myself that I needed professional help. I was willing to do anything just to make the pain stop. I went to see a secular psychiatrist. I have to admit, she looked about as crazy as I felt. She charged $100 an hour for me to sit in a chair and pour my heart out to her. She could not offer an eternal solution, only worldly philosophies. She had me blaming everybody. She opened wounds further that she couldn't close. She left me stripped bare with no hope of conquering this thing or getting a grip on these unstable emotions that I carried. What I did not know then, but know now, is that she couldn't help me. For in order for me to be set free of the present, I would need to be released from the guilt of the past, and only Jesus Christ could give me that freedom. John 8:36, states *"If the Son, therefore, shall make you free, ye shall be free indeed."* That is the best and only counseling one can offer.

Jean felt sorry for me, but could offer no solution at that point. Besides, she was a source of the problem. She and my mother were generally the main focus at the sessions.

Paul said in <u>Romans 7:19</u> *"For the good that I would, I do not; but the evil which I would not, that I do."* After a while, I wanted out of the homosexual lifestyle, but I did not know how to let this thing go, it was too gripping. *I will not mislead you into thinking that I did not like the feelings that came with the sexual activities. I enjoyed the "thrill," and the emotional "highs," but in the years to come, the "lows" made the highs not worth it. I was in sin and it was pleasurable, but only for a season.*

<u>Hebrews 11:24-25</u> states *"By faith Moses, when he was come to years, refused to be called the son of Pharaoh's daughter; Choosing rather to suffer affliction with the people of God than to enjoy the pleasures of sin for a season."*

Even in my mess, I knew I was wrong but I dared not publicize it. It would just be my secret for a while. Because I was covering my sin, I would not and could not prosper (Proverbs 28:13). I could not move forward in a life that would please God.

Even in recent years, I'm at times plagued with depression. When I first typed this chapter, in 1997, I experienced a dark moment in my life. In July 1997, I had been laid-off from my job, just two weeks prior to having foot surgery. There I was jobless, mounting medical bills and receiving only $176.00 weekly from Unemployment Compensation (I had been receiving a $687.50 weekly income). It was a dark moment and one of Satan's smaller imps whispered sweet nothings into my ear - *"go ahead take those pain pills from your surgery."* I had to bring every thought into captivity, into obedience. As it states in <u>II Corinthians 10:4-5</u>, *"For the weapons of our warfare are not carnal, but mighty through God to the pulling down of strongholds. Casting down imaginations, and every high thing that exalteth itself against the knowledge of God, and bringing into captivity every thought to the obedience of Christ."* I gave God the thanks and the praise for my deliverance and flushed every one of those pain pills down the toilet. I had to take this thing by *force.*

It was also during this time of unemployment that the Lord had given me a second book, but the first one (this one) had not been published yet. I experienced a great spiritual warfare of the mind, dealing with depression. I had to begin to claim God's promises for my life. This practice was a must for me during low points. The very thing that the Lord has set you free from, I believe if one becomes weak, that thing intensifies. That is why we must keep on the *armor of God*, and never leave home without it. Never ever think we can't fall again. I Corinthians 10:12 states *"Wherefore, let him that thinketh he standeth take heed lest he fall."*

The holes grew bigger!

Haggai 1:5-6 says *"Now, therefore, thus saith the Lord of hosts: Consider your ways. Ye have sown much, and bring in little; ye eat, but ye have not enough; ye drink, but ye are not filled with drink; ye clothe yourselves, but there is none warm; and he that earneth wages earneth wages to put it into a bag with holes."*

As a child, I was never encouraged by my mother to save money. Tithing was certainly foreign. College was not discussed, so there were no goals to meet. In elementary school, however, the teachers taught the students how to open up a savings account. My first savings account was opened at PSFS (Philadelphia Savings Fund Society), located in Philadelphia, Pennsylvania. Each week I would put my little pennies into the account. However, because it was not taught at home, I was not consistent and would soon lose interest in saving. In high school I began again, but would soon become inconsistent again. Saving is a lesson that has to be taught early so consistency and commitment can be developed.

During my late teens when I had obtained a full-time job, I would once again make the attempt to save. I had become pretty financially sound for a young-adult person. But because of lack of training and direction in finances, I began to spend my money like there was no tomorrow. It was nothing for me to pay a $100 for a pair of shoes. And I would spend that on Jean as well or anyone else for that matter. By 1985, my sinful lifestyle had left me thousands of dollars in debt, and what seemed to be no light at the end of the tunnel. I didn't spend it all on Jean, but my judgment in spending and managing money had been clouded by the lifestyle that I was living.

It took me realizing that what I had belonged to God. Proverbs 3:9-10 says, *"Honor the Lord with thy substance, and with the first fruits of all thine increase; So shall thy barns be filled with plenty, and thy presses shall burst out with new wine."*

Proverbs 22:7 says *"The rich ruleth over the poor, and the borrower is servant to the lender."* My finances during this time were in complete shambles. I was $6,000.00 in debt and God in His sovereignty delivered me in one and a half years (one of his many miracles) and from that day forward I vowed to cut-up my charge cards and use cash only; unfortunately years later, (in the late nineties), due to unemployment, medical expenses, etc., I slipped back into poor financial mismanagement. I'm currently digging out, but this time I have a strong foundation built on financial management and soon will be debt free.

Look at me!

Along with physical, mental and financial issues, I also had emotional issues that needed to be addressed.

In Junior High School, I was voted "class clown." Now that is nothing to be proud of, but that's what got me attention. So it worked for me! I think that I have a pretty good sense of humor and can be very witty, but it is much tempered now. I always liked to make people laugh, it is a natural for me and I don't have to work too hard for the results. So often while growing up, I was sad and very depressed. So it was always good for me to see somebody else laughing. If my talents had been cultivated, I probably would have been a stand-up comedian or actress; it's never too late though.

Even today, I must constantly place my need for *affirmation* and *attention* before the Lord. In doing this, the wanting can't easily slip up on me. During the preparation of this chapter in 1997, at a weekend Women's Advance, some of the *need for attention residue* slipped up on me. I acted like a spoiled brat wanting attention from a dear friend of mine. But because she is a dear friend, she called me to the carpet on this behavior.

The Lord has shown me that I am delivered, but to be mindful of speaking constantly a word of affirmation from His Word, Jeremiah 31:3 states *"The Lord hath appeared of old unto me, saying, Yea, I have loved thee with an everlasting love; therefore, with loving kindness have I drawn thee."* Speaking scriptures that remind me of His presence and nearness to me, Psalms 46:1,*"God is our refuge and strength, a very present help in trouble."* Scriptures of his faithfulness, Lamentations 3:22-23, *"It is because of the Lord's mercies that we are not consumed, because his compassions fail not. They are new every morning; great is thy faithfulness."*

Another thing that the Lord showed me is how important it is as a child to have that strong foundation of affirmation and affection laid, or else the foundation crumbles under the weight of wanting. And building upon a broken foundation is difficult, virtually impossible. Temporary structures often crumble under excessive weights as well. The foundation has to be destroyed and rebuilt.

Does this meet your approval?

It was up until the last few years, that I had found myself seeking continuously the approval of others. I was always wondering what people thought, whether the things that God had directed me to do would ruffle someone's feathers. Or even worst afraid to walk in what God has destined me for because of other people's opinions.

Oftentimes, I was subjected to doing things alone as a child. Later years would bring problems in building relational bonds for me. You'd be surprised at the impact that just making cookies with a child could have on them later in life. It teaches children how to be a team player, how to listen and follow instructions, and also how to build relationships.

My shyness was a result of learning no relational and communication skills from my mother. Children need to know that they are special and a priority. I thought that I had to do things for people so that I could be special or liked by them.

The weakness in the *Choleric-Melancholy* temperament is that the "*Choleric* is domineering and possessive, while the *Melancholy* is pessimistic (you don't love me, if you loved me...)" states Tim LaHaye ("Spirit-Controlled Temperament"; Tyndale House Publishers, Inc.; Revised Edition 1992). So during my years of adolescence, depression, and isolation these characteristics were battling against one another and each one winning.

I believe many schizophrenics are melancholy people. Elijah (I Kings 19) had a melancholy temperament. Why else would he want to hide under a juniper tree and die? Sure pessimism had made its way into Elijah's spirit and he forgot who God said that he was. He ultimately wanted Jezebel's approval. She hated him and wanted him dead. Elijah trembled at the thought, causing him to run.

Because I was always trying to get someone's approval, I made poor life changing decisions based on that need. I'm reminded of a very small church in the suburbs of Pennsylvania that I joined several years ago. The church was in the midst of a major transition and a heated court battle surfaced. This was a church in which I always felt that I needed someone's approval, especially the pastor's. I felt that I did nothing right in his sight. I had a couple encounters with the pastor. I would certainly not call them counseling sessions for I was not the better for it. Each one left me further destroyed and distraught. He was my leader and whatever he said I thought was right. The verbal abuse that was displayed left me with a feeling of nothingness, that everything I did was not meeting up to his expectations, and that there was no hope for me. I no longer respected him as a pastor or a man. *I vowed not to go in his office alone again!*

I can now see how people get caught up in a *cult*. There is a thin line between caring and control. I wanted to submit but this was an abusive, controlling, insensitive, and non-motivating environment. There were power struggles and my opinion was not welcomed. I was not being built-up, but torn down, striped of all the life and hope I had left. Sermons became no more than an *"injection of a spirit destroying venom." And yes even the homosexuals were there!*

Jeremiah 23:1, 2b, 4 states *"Woe be unto the shepherds who destroy and scatter the sheep of my pasture saith the Lord.... Behold, I will visit upon you the evil of your doings, saith the Lord. And I will set up shepherds over them who shall feed them; and they shall fear no more, nor be dismayed, neither shall they be lacking, saith the Lord."*

With all the confusion and schism going on at that church, the sheep began to scatter. The remaining people begun to look lifeless, like robots. They reminded me of the Dunkin Donut Man, *"time to make the donuts" — time to go to church - time to worship.* I would get spurts of excitement with Jesus, because He was doing something in my life outside of those four walls.

During this time, I was doing short-term missions trips, and I was strengthened with a boldness to stand up and fight. God had a destiny and a calling on my life that I had to get to, no matter what it took. This became my posture, *"Don't mess with me God has brought me through too much for you to play with me. Don't get in my way, where God is taking me, you may get run over."*

During the time when the church court battle started I was on another missions trip. When I returned I knew it was time for me to go. I would never go forth in Jesus in that environment; it was not profitable for me. I had to be sober and vigilant. I had to stand strong. I had to know that this was God's battle, not mine. I had to remain confident in God's work in my life and plan for my life. The environment was a stronghold, one that produced low expectations from God. Based on what the pastor had spoken into my life, I even thought God didn't approve of me. Now that's hopeless!

I knew that I was in a legalistic, rigid environment of tradition. *Max Lucado* puts it this way: "*Legalism* is a dark world. ...*Legalism* is slow torture, suffocation of the spirit, amputation of one's dreams. *Legalism* is just enough religion to keep you, but not enough to nourish you. So you starve. Your teachers don't know where to go for food, so you starve together. Your diet is rules and standards. No vitamins. No taste. No zest. Just bland, predictable religion. ...It's rigid. It's uniform. It's mechanical - and it's not from God. ...*Legalism* puts the fear of man in you. It makes you approval-hungry. You become keenly aware of what others will say and think, and you do what it takes to please them. Conformity is not fun, but it's safe. The uniform doesn't fit, but it's approved, so you wear it. You don't know why you are marching or where you are going. But who are you to ask questions? So you stay in step and plod down the path of least resistance." (*He Still Moves Stones*, Max Lucado, 1993, Word Publishing, Dallas Texas, pp 128-130).

I had to pray my way through this thing. I had to count it all joy. It was coming to the realization that these trials and circumstances were working something in me and out of me. The trials and circumstances were just fertilizers - used to make me grow. *"A stronger prayer life and boldness would grow out of this trial."*

I've often heard my pastor as well as other pastors say, *"if you can't support the vision, then you need to leave the church."* There was no vision being executed there. I was on a ship that had no sail, being tossed to and fro. The ship would soon capsize and all the passengers would go overboard. I had to jump ship!

DELIVERANCE

DELIVERANCE

> Any healthy and thriving plant has been freed of all trappings, received the right amount of sunlight, plenty of water and a good nutritional supplement for its growing process.

Let me start by saying that my God is gracious and merciful and every time I think of how He covered me and protected me in the midst of every sexual act that I performed, I'm convinced that He must have always had a plan for my life. Why else would He allow me to remain? To walk out of that lifestyle and be *"AIDS FREE,"* I know that there is a testimony and a ministry to follow. Coming out of the *"other closet"* is not easy but it can be done. The *"other closet"* is the closet of a restrained, repented and changed heterosexual lifestyle.

Coming out of the "other closet" is an extreme task. For in coming out and confessing change, it creates a conflict with your present relationships. You loose your identity because now you take on another one. Your relationships will most likely end because you are no longer with the homosexual crowd. You are now probably going to have to establish a new emotional network. It is just as hard coming out of the "other closet" as it is coming out of the first one.

Homosexuality is a behavior that can be stopped. I Corinthians 6:9-11 states *"Know ye not that the unrighteous shall not inherit the kingdom of God? Be not deceived: neither fornicators, nor idolaters, nor adulterers, nor effeminate, nor abusers of themselves with mankind, Nor thieves, nor covetous, nor drunkards, nor revilers, nor extortioners, shall inherit the kingdom of God. And such were some of you; but ye are washed, but ye are sanctified, but ye are justified in the name of the Lord Jesus, and by the Spirit of our God."*

There is a way out of this thing, for you see *"All have sinned, and come short of the glory of God,"* Romans 3:23. And I imagine that you think because you're in sin God does not love you, *"But God commendeth his love toward us in that, while we were yet sinners, Christ died for us,"* <u>Romans 5:8</u>. It is just a matter of you believing, receiving and confessing. That love is already waiting and available for you; *"....if thou shalt confess with thy mouth the Lord Jesus, and shalt believe in thine heart that God hath raised him from the dead, thou shalt be saved. For with the heart man believeth unto righteousness; and with the mouth confession is made unto salvation,"* <u>Romans 10: 9-10</u>.

After eight years the Lord opened my prison bars and set me free. It was only afterwards that I realized the key was in my cage of pain. **The "*key*" was to submit my will, and the "*key*" was my confession."**

Getting out was not easy and I don't want you to think that it was. But, God was and still is faithful. One step for sure was to cut all ties with Jean. No phone calls, no visits, nothing. It was very lonely for I had depended on Jean for my every emotional need and affirmation. I was afraid that I could not live without her. There were times when I called or visited. There was what felt like a *hole* in my heart. But, the love of God filled it. It took time. Eventually I had no desire to be around Jean. God had taken away my desires for a lesbian relationship, to put it bluntly, the taste was now gone.

I have come to realize that I was dead to sin; therefore I did not have to live in it any longer. The Bible says in <u>Romans 6</u> - *(v.1-2)"What shall we say then? Shall we continue in sin, that grace may abound? God forbid. How shall we, that are dead to sin, live any longer in it? (v.4) Therefore, we are buried with him by baptism into death, that as Christ was raised up from the dead by the glory of the Father, even so we also should walk in newness of life. (v.6-7) Knowing this, that our old man is crucified with him, that the body of sin might be destroyed, that henceforth we should not serve sin. For he that is dead is freed from sin. (v.11-13) Likewise, reckon ye also yourselves to be dead indeed unto sin, but alive unto God through Jesus Christ, our Lord. Let not sin, therefore, reign in your mortal body, that ye should obey it in its lusts. Neither yield ye your members as instruments of unrighteousness unto sin, but yield yourselves unto God, as those that are alive from the dead, and your members as instruments of righteousness unto God."*

I had also come to realize how my lifestyle was breaking the very heart of God. My Creator, my Father, the one that made me, and then saved me. Remember how it felt when you were a child and waited for your favorite aunt, uncle or even your mother or father to come and take you somewhere and they never showed up? Your heart was broken; you were disappointed. In more recent years the imprint of God's disappointment in my former lifestyle has become very vivid. I have seen God hovering over my sin-stained life, drops of tears falling down; whispering out, "don't you know what I have purposed for your life?" "Do you know what I want to do through you?"

As a child you had rules and guidelines to follow in your home and when you violated those rules and guidelines, your parents were disappointed with you. They thought that you knew better and that you trusted their judgment. That's how God feels when He has given His all for us and then we violate the plan and order that he has established for us to live by. The violation says that we don't trust His judgment.

Matthew 5:30a, states *"And if thy right hand offend thee, cut it off, and cast it from thee."* It takes *cutting off* immediately that relationship - no phone calls, no visits, no nothing! You need a person to encourage you during this time, to hold you accountable. I didn't have that accountability, no one knew, other than Jean, and she was not going to hold me accountable. I made myself busy in church work, which was unhealthy. I became spiritually burned out. It was a temporary solution. Church work did not allow me to spend time by myself with God, for God to show me, *me*. There has to be a balance.

The Body of Christ plays an important role in a homosexual's deliverance. The saddest commentary is that most church leaders, pastors, etc. don't understand how to reach the homosexual community. Unfortunately, there are sometimes *"just as many homosexuals in the pulpit as in the pews."* And with churches catering especially to the homosexual community, the previous statement holds true more and more.

In non-homosexual churches, there are often off-colored jokes, and inappropriate comments made about homosexuals. But it's nothing to laugh about. The very moment that a joke is made a wall goes up in the homosexual who may have been at the point of reaching out for help. They retreat, feeling that people will make fun of them. No other sin is so ostracized or exploited. Please don't think that I'm giving justification for the homosexual to remain in sin, by no means. But as believers, we do have to prepare an environment or atmosphere set for change. One that promotes compassion and change, not bitterness and rejection.

Homosexuality is a bondage, a destructive lifestyle, and only God and the aid of His Holy Spirit can bring someone out. There also must be an *"act of the will"* to want to come out, to want a change. (Pride has to be banished as well, that attitude of I'm not doing anything wrong has to go.) I ached so much during my time in the lesbian lifestyle that I just knew there had to be another way of life. John 8:36 says "*If the Son, therefore, shall make you free, ye shall be free indeed.*"

First there must be peace made with God. Second the peace of God must be cultivated, through an intimate relationship with Him. Isaiah 26:3, "*Thou wilt keep him in perfect peace, whose mind is stayed on thee, because he trusteth in thee.*"

A preacher can talk until he's blue in the face about homosexuality, but until the person realizes that the sin crushes the very heart of God, no change will take place and that of course is with any sin.

Somehow homosexuality is rated the #1 Sin. (Although, I must say that in today's media it ranks as being the #1 O.K. thing to do.) People in the church can say "I do drugs" - we'll help them. But let a person say "I'm gay," then they're shunned. It's not communicable. If you touch a homosexual you won't die. But that is how homosexuals are treated.

This reaction I believe further hinders a homosexual's deliverance. They may be on the brink of wanting out, but may not have any help or support.

I had a friend up North who was in and out of the lifestyle. His church just did not know how to minister to him. My friend was a faithful leader in the church, just burned out. He had gotten out of the church and was trying to get it together, but he was weak and around weak folks. Many times he tried to walk right, probably that was the problem, he tried, and didn't allow the Holy Spirit to assist. Oftentimes he would call me crying when he was working on getting his life straight.

One night I told him that the Lord had delivered me from a homosexual lifestyle. There was complete silence on the other end of the phone and I thought that he had passed out. He was stunned! I shared with him my testimony and what God had done for me. At that time I knew that he knew that there was hope for him. Sad to say though that today that hope has not transcended his flesh. With nowhere to turn, he turned back into the lifestyle, leaving many broken strings in family relationships. The leadership at his church missed the signs.

No one would walk with him through the restoration process, or to be honest with him about where they were with the issue of homosexuality. No one would be honest with him where they may have been in their current relationship with God, or issues they may have struggled with in their walk with the Lord. (But in all honesty, I can't blame it all on his church, for at this point in his life, he was not trying to come out. He was comfortable.) Initially the church did not know how to meet him where he was which caused him to become discouraged and to stray. Instead, they were condemning him in words and even in their actions.

Most churches are not equipped to handle homosexuals. I'm not saying they don't have the Word (although some don't) but in some of the churches they just don't know how to restore. **Restoration is preached, but seldom is it put into practice**. The church holds the great weight of fault on our shoulders. Very few churches have effective ministries set up that minister to those struggling with homosexuality or sexual identity. Or if it does, it is a well-kept secret, quietly announced, or a little blurb in the church bulletin, or Christian education catalog.

We are the moral standard, right? Then the body of Christ needs to stand up. Aren't you tired of perpetrators, pretending practitioners, and people posing as something they are not?

Homosexuals require a compassionate person to walk with them, not a condemning person. You see, I knew I was wrong, that my life was being lived in error. I did not have to have that pointed out. What I needed though was someone to tell me how to get out; what steps to take. No one knew except Jean. So it was God and God alone that brought me out. He *wooed* me to himself. He gave me a love no one else could give. He listened to me and He encouraged me. Then He sent people who loved me just as I was. He loved me with an everlasting love. We should all dare to walk in the compassion of Christ.

It will sometimes take a delivered homosexual to draw another homosexual out. This person has been there. They are more sensitive to the emotional and spiritual needs of the person. You do develop somewhat of a *seventh sense*, a *radar* if you will, to people that are homosexuals. It's that spirit that you sense. It makes it easier for you to develop that friendship and rapport with them, a rapport that will allow you to *hear* where they are.

Some pastor's will talk about homosexuality, but they don't tell you how to get out. I'll walk you through this thing. Establishing a ministry or support group specifically for persons struggling with homosexuality is so crucial. But pastors sometimes are so busy telling homosexuals about the sin, that they don't give any solutions or directions for coming out of the lifestyle.

Trust me, homosexuality is not a sin inside the church where you will get too many people raising their hands and saying yes, I've been there. The world though is audacious in speaking out where they are. We will admit to divorce, drugs, fornication, debt, maybe adultery, stealing and lying. But homosexuality - Oh God, what will people think!

I have some other acquaintances up North that are struggling with homosexuality, but I know that the environment that they are in is not going to help them out. Mind you they are in good bible teaching churches, but they will never be challenged out of the lifestyle. Not unless, like God did with me, (He pulled me out - literally dragging me by the feet). God had somewhere for me to go and something for me to do and He was not going to wait on man to get me there.

A ministry for homosexuals has to be handled completely differently than a ministry for drug abuse, spousal abuse, rape, or any other cruel act towards the body. *"It is a stronghold that captures and holds hostage the whole being - mind, body and soul."* You eat, sleep and breathe this lifestyle.

You actually will have to be de-programmed. Many individuals in homosexual lifestyles have never been taught how a man or woman acts. Their parents probably never knew how a man or woman should act, therefore, they did not have anything to teach the child. I'm not just talking about a man who puts on pants and a woman who puts on a dress. I'm talking about men teaching their sons how to respect women, to love them, to pull chairs out, to protect them, etc. I'm talking about women teaching their daughters how to respect men, to love them, to submit to them, to encourage them, to take care of them, and to nurture, etc.

Once I decided to present my body to be a living sacrifice, (Romans 12:1-2 - *"I beseech you therefore brethren, by the mercies of God, that ye present your bodies a living sacrifice, holy, acceptable unto God, which is your reasonable service. And be not conformed to this world, but be ye transformed by the renewing of your mind, that ye may prove what is that good, and acceptable, and perfect, will of God,"*) God began renewing my mind. He gave me a peace unlike anything that I had experienced before (Isaiah 26:3). I w*illed* to want to change. Those two words *"I Will"*, are activators of action to anything you want to do in life, good, bad or ugly.

Ironically, after coming out, I became bitter towards the homosexual community. I did not have any compassion. I said if I could get out of it so could you. It was only within the last few years that God dealt with me about it. He said to me *"how can you dare turn your back on people that you once shared the same lifestyle with?"* *"I'm going to use your past mess as a witness and testimony that will bring deliverance to them."* It was then that I knew that I had a ministry to the homosexuals. It was who God had joined me to - the burden, the passion and reason for living was to reach the homosexual.

It hit close to home with my family. I have a cousin who currently lives with his lover. My anger with them was that they both think that it's all right. They actively take part in church, they are prominent members — faithful. They have a home and business together. The church just accepts them as dedicated members, never challenging their sin state. They are accepted as a couple who cares for one another, in the church, in the family.

I must now speak hope and life to the homosexual. I must draw them out if they are willing to go. *I've been to hell - I know what it's like. I've met the people. It's an all-consuming fire!*

If you are in the lifestyle or perhaps someone you know, this is the challenge: Ask yourself, "Where am I going? Is my life right now, today, profiting me? Is my life pleasing to God?" Assess the condition of your life right now. If you are honest, you'll probably answer - it's a *wreck*, full of confusion and pain.

> *To the homosexual who is reading this and you have come to the end of yourself (your agenda, plans, and way of doing things):* "You're not alone. I have prayed for you long before you received this book. My prayers even now are being directed towards you. And where I can't be, God is! Look over your shoulders, in front of you, beside you, under you, above you. He's there! Just accept His love and forgiveness."

<u>I John 1:9</u> says *"If we confess our sins, he is faithful and just to forgive us our sins, and to cleanse us from all unrighteousness."*

A CALL TO GROW TO EXCELLENCE

A CALL TO GROW TO EXCELLENCE

> Once any plant or crop has been set free from anything that traps and hinders growth, it will be released to grow freely with no hindrances or obstructions.

At this point of my life, around the mid-eighties, I was lonely and afraid. I had pretty much isolated myself from my family; I felt that they didn't care for me and I sure did not care for them. During these times Aunt Dee (as she is so fondly known) lived next door to the apartment I was now living in. She was not my blood aunt but I had adopted most of her family as my extended family; and even to this day, she is still Aunt Dee to me.

Often she would challenge me to submit to the Holy Spirit. I was not familiar with this terminology and I was always baffled when she said this. However, her words kept prodding at my spirit more than she would ever know.

You see I had been delivered from the *acts of homosexuality*, but I had not been *healed of the scars* that the lifestyle left. I had not cast down my imaginations, nor brought into captivity any of my thoughts (II Corinthians 10:5). I had not yet learned who I was in Christ Jesus. I had not been endowed with the Joshua spirit (Joshua 1: 6-7). I was twenty-five years old now and something was still missing in my life. I had not accepted God's forgiveness. I had now been through abuse, rejection, pornography, isolation, homosexuality and sickness. All had left their mark on my life!

In 1985, there was an acquaintance of mine that kept inviting me to her church for a visit. She said that they had this young, dynamite teacher, and she was absolutely right.

Initially, I was somewhat scared to accept the invite. I was still in a store-front church that had strong family ties. By then, I had been in that storefront church for fourteen years. Although it was not meeting my spiritual needs, I just couldn't break those ties. What would everybody think? Would my family cut me off? I questioned myself day after day. But I wanted something different; I needed something different. I accepted the invite.

The first visit was a Sunday in July of 1985, which revolutionized my life! The service was upbeat and the choir sang songs that had words from something other than a hymnbook. At a Wednesday night Bible Study in August 1985, I would re-dedicate my life back to the Lord. I returned what was His anyway. I had taken the first step to submitting.

That week a revival was going on. After bible study, I stayed for the services. The message was *"Neighbor, for all you do this bud's for you,"* Numbers 17: 1-8, preached by Dr. Clarence Walker. That message offered a *ray of hope* in my dark life.

The next day I was to go in for pre-admission testing to have my thyroid removed. When I arrived, the doctor said that my thyroid function had returned to normal and my Sarcoid was in remission. Well I've been in remission now for over fifteen years. I had just experienced my first of many healings to come. No more blood work! No more hospital visits! Hospital visits had consumed three-quarters of my life for 2 years. In August 1985, I returned to a somewhat normal life (I had to find a job, I had not worked for 2 years.) I was not excited to go to work. *At first I was afraid, I was petrified, thinking I could not survive. But oh no, not I, I did survive!*

I was getting Bible teaching that I never had before. I began to learn about the Holy Spirit's work in the believer's life and about the Church (Body of Christ) in general. I began to grow by leaps and bounds. The word had begun to take root in my life. From that church, a foundation was laid, upon which many years of building would take place. I became very active in ministry (Sunday School, Audio Ministry, Evangelism Ministry, Choir, Youth Ministry).

Although being under the Word, I still was messed up from previous relationships that had left many scars. I was, I guess you could say, on the rebound. I was still missing a true representation of love. I began to fall (plunge) into ungodly relationships with different men. There was never sexual intercourse, but trust me, there was everything that led up to the act; the passionate kissing, fondling, etc.

These relationships stripped me further of my self-worth. I slipped into another bondage that was hard to get out of as well. The same behavior patterns took form. The buying of expensive gifts, being controlled by the relationship and allowing the men to control and toy with my emotions. Wanting to do everything that I could to please them. I placed myself once again into relationships that would use me both physically and mentally and begin to destroy spiritually what was being established.

I found deliverance and healing when I was able to confess the past and present to my then, *Prayer Partner* on May 23, 1992. James 5:16a, *"Confess your faults one to another, and pray one for another, that you may be healed."* It brought such freedom; she was the very first of a few that I had been able to confess my homosexual lifestyle to. Each time that I had shared it there would be more freedom, openness and more liberation.

She had such a grab on the throne of God, sadly though it seems that she just was unable to grab enough to climb out of her own pit of despair. She herself lacked affirmation and had unhealthy relationships. She has experienced much pain and still is, right in her own home, her own mind, a prisoner.

Years were spent going to seminars, conferences, retreats and the such. I was eventually delivered of those ungodly relationships. Jesus had begun to take first priority in my life. Having a man in my life didn't matter. I was getting too close to Jesus. I was learning to let him be the man in my life. There would be in later years a few men that I had tried to establish relationships with but they did not go very far.

One man was passive. He had no spiritual goals and was not motivated to say the least, in his career direction. He also struggled with masturbation and would only be a huge distraction in blue jeans.

Another man would come along that had an *angry spirit*. We often got into screaming matches. (My old nature had not quite been tamed and I did not have any problem stepping to him.) He was not a communicator and did not want to address issues. He possessed an *ostrich spirit*, one that would keep his head in the sand (don't challenge me, I don't see the need attitude). He also would lie. When we initially met he said that he was debt free, only to find out that he had a school debt of a few thousand dollars. To further complicate things, he was not paying on the debt. I called him on it and he felt because he was not making a lot of money, he did not have to pay it.

I soon came to realize that I was establishing a pattern of unqualified men for my life. It would be Jesus and me until He brought the right *"Adam."* The one that He has breathed life into and has fashioned me for. There have also been a couple of men that I was interested in, but the interest was not mutual.

One gentleman is a minister up North, I was very interested in him. I was drawn to his spirit; it was a hearty one. He had the gift of exhortation. I believed the interest was mutual but he did not pursue. I'm from the old school in that respect, I don't go looking, you come and find me. <u>Proverbs 18:22</u>, *"Whoso findeth a wife findeth a good thing, and obtaineth favor from the Lord,"* contrary to what the modern dating method says.

I was still getting to know Jesus, He already knew me. I thought it behooved me to get to know him. I'm really glad that I did!

I had and still am directing my focus towards getting closer to Him until that time that God sees fit to bless me. *NO, I DON'T HAVE THE GIFT OF SINGLE-*

NESS, AND I DON'T CLAIM IT EITHER. Cause honey, there are some men up in New Birth - and I mean some *"sho'-nuff"* men! I love a well-dressed, good smelling man, amongst other things (saved, well built, job - you get the picture). A strong warrior type sends my spirit soaring, yet tender enough to weep in the presence of the Almighty God, and humble enough to submit to the God of his life. And because my *"spiritual father,"* Bishop Long exudes this type of life before me, I won't be confused about what I see.

Many challenges in my walk took place, and many choices had to be made to stand or not to stand. Yearly I would attend the Youth in Basic Life Conflict Seminar. These seminars changed areas in my life one at a time.

It was also during one of these seminars that God challenged me to resolve the conflict between my mother and I. I called her and ask her to forgive me for being rebellious and having such a bad attitude as a teenager. Her response was, "that we all make mistakes." I was not quite looking for that type of response, but I realized at that point that my mother just did not know how to reach out and love me. She was never taught. She raised me to the best of her ability, what she knew. I had to accept that! It was very hard at first. I wanted to be a part of the mother and daughter events that took place in churches and at community functions. I wanted to go to the malls with my mother, take a weekend get-away and spend money. However, life does not stand still, so neither could I stand in that spot of wanting. I had to move in order to grow.

Grow, I say, Grow!

Psalms 1:3a, *"And he shall be like a tree planted by the rivers of water, that bringeth forth its fruit in its season…"* This was a season of much growth for me. However, my fruit began to get stale, my life was stagnant. I was being pushed into another dimension. I needed a new challenge, to be able to branch out. I needed to be where the Word of God was not only taught, but lived in the lives of the people. I needed the Word to come alive! No compromise, no low standards and no more tradition!

Circumstances and situations would bring me to Atlanta, believing that God was going to do something so miraculous in my life and I waited in expectation for the manifestation of it. Psalms 62:5, *"My soul, wait thou only upon God; for my expectation is from him."*

On July 7, 1996, I joined New Birth Missionary Baptist Church, where Bishop Eddie L. Long is the Senior Pastor. Jeremiah 3:15 states *"And I will give you pastors according to mine heart, who shall feed you with knowledge and understanding."*

The New Birth experience has been an explosive demonstration of God for me. The Word received by the Bishop weekly has revolutionized my life, healing has taken place, scars have been healed, liberation has come about.

"WATCH THIS, WATCH THIS, WATCH THIS!!"

I have seen the Word come alive in my life as well as in the lives of other church members. I've seen people healed; people's mortgages get paid (now how many churches have you gone to that a person's mortgage was paid during service). I've seen people come to the altar and lay down cigarettes. I've seen homosexuals come to the altar because they want to be set free. I've seen people just give property to the church. I've seen projects come in production - not ten years down the line but right now. I've witnessed 100, 200 and almost 300 hundred people joining in one Sunday; almost 2,000 or more join in one quarter (some churches don't even have that many members). People will sit in traffic for an hour trying to get in (I know this for a fact, I've been caught in that myself). I've seen boldness reach a new height in me. Confidence has taken a front seat, fear has taken a back seat. I've experienced a new anointing in my life. I speak up and out!

The Lord has used Bishop Long to speak life into me once again. You see when I came to New Birth, I was a walking dead person, depending on a life support system to sustain me. I had had a *cardiac arrest* and the Holy Spirit used Bishop to resuscitate me through the word, *pumping* the word of life into me one scripture at a time. Positive affirmation, healing, hope, courage, joy, peace and boldness were pumped. I began to feel all the *tubes* of guilt, hurt and shame fall off. I am now disconnected from the machines, I'm now breathing on my own.

You see, I am no longer bound. All the *trappings* of my life have been cut off. I'm free to grow, grow, grow. This is just the beginning of my fruit harvest. For this is the way that I was born, to grow and be productive. To bring glory and honor to the farmer (Jesus Christ), the one who has given me water, food, sunlight, protection, and life.

Jeremiah 29:11, *"For I know the thoughts that I think toward you, saith the Lord, thoughts of peace, and not of evil, to give you an expected end."*

ABOUT THE AUTHOR

ABOUT THE AUTHOR

Jacqueline Lamar was born and raised in Philadelphia, PA. She is a graduate of Beulah New Life Bible Institute, and received a certificate from the Evangelical Training Association (ETA) in June 1996.

Ms. Lamar is a member of New Birth Missionary Baptist Church located in Lithonia, GA under the pastorate of Bishop Eddie L. Long.

Since 1997, Ms. Lamar has been lecturer and teacher of a Spiritual Warfare class on Homosexuality. In September 2001, Ms. Lamar began teaching a class titled "Love Me, I'm Different" through the "New Birth School of Life Institute (Christian Education)." *I Wasn't Born This Way,* her first published work, is considered a major contemporary Christian teaching tool addressing relevant issues to overcome spiritual brokenness.

Available soon is a Teacher's Guide for those persons, groups or ministries interested in offering solid restoration ministry principals to those struggling to be spiritually free from the bondage of homosexuality and other alternative lifestyles. Ms. Lamar is also available for speaking engagements, seminars and conferences and book clubs. For additional information and extra copies of this book contact: Jacqueline R. Lamar, P.O. Box 1472, Lithonia, GA 30058 or via the author's e-mail at: jacauthor@juno.com.